WHY
YOU ARE
HERE

Novel

KARTHIKA S NAIR

Karthika S. Nair

Born in modest circumstances in a small village Manjoor   at Kottayam. She completed her post-graduation in physics from Kuriakose Elias College Mamanam and working as an online teacher in a leading private firm Guardian Online. Published some novelettes and short stories in online publishing platform pratilipi. "Her spouse MR. Akhil S. Nair is working as a manager in South Indian Bank and daughter Ishani Karthika Akhil is a student of Bharathiya Vidhya Bhavan Thirunavaya.

Address:
Vathappallil House,
Memury P.O., Kuruppanthara
Kottayam. Pin 686611

Mob:7034369288
karthikasofficial@gmal.com

Dedication

To my husband, Akhil S Nair,
who persistently give suggetions
to my works

WHY
YOU ARE
HERE

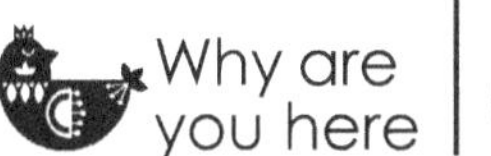

Why are
you here
6

1
Why you are here

Why you are here?
A person looked like a sage with a long moustache combined with beard asked with a murmuring voice.
Why everyone is here?
She looked at his long beard having both silver and black hairs.
She doesn't want to answer.
She deeply digging something in her mind. As he noted her shallow face and deep-rooted thoughts he stops talking and take a large breath with hookah placed near to his face.
She tries to divert her thoughts by thinking about the sage.
He may be educated, that visible in his face. She feels that the person whom Infront of her may be a business man who totally frustrated at a point of life and just came her to escape from reality.
Do you want this?
He tries to pull the hookah towards her
What is this?
Take a puff and you will get the answer of the question
Which question?
The one you have in your mind for the past decades.
She scrutinized him. what do you mean?
He smiled with his eyes.
Are you in search of an answer.?
How do you know that?
She became a little frustrated.
Because you are always answering with questions.

She paused for a while. Yes. maybe I am answering by questions, how does it mean that I am in search of a question?

This a mysterious valley of God Siva and there are so many questions you may want to ask but no one can answer it completely.

The sage wakeup from the large stone near to her and start walking.

When she noticed that he was departing ,she followed him.

Wait. I am coming with you.

He didn't seem to hear that. She rushed to reach near him. But when she looked down in search of her sandals, and look back to the sage she found that the sage was disappeared. She stood there,it may be a great opportunity to discuss my life with him. But I missed it.

Again, she sat near to a Yamuna River, the cold water of sacred Yamuna flowing by chanting the mantra

Om…namah sivaya..om namah sivaya..om…..

She feels some kind of spirituality and she want to spend the whole day there but because of the number of people approaching to that area she lost her privacy and try to shift to some other area, While her mind moving with the rhythm om ..om..om..

She is Nayamika, a Nurse working at an old age home in Uttarakhand.

Why Nayamika decided to go for a devotional journey to Kedarnath alone?

Still Nayamika was also thinking about that, why she wants to go.

She actually doesn't try to dig deeply in mind because she knows when she enclaving any pebble from any point, it completely destroys her sand palace and an avalanche of destruction occurs.

So, she just obeying her subconscious mind without asking why I want to do so.

She believes in her subconscious mind, which leads her.

She was in a state of mind, that she doesn't understand. She was thinking something, but it isn't recalled by her brain.

Only the thing she can realize is that she is not happy, not triumphant

Why am I not happy?

How can I make myself happy?

Am I not satisfied with my present life?

2

In search of finding her

I want to talk to the sage who can predict future
Nayamika enquired to the group of saints who sat on the opening
of an ancient looking cave.
They had shown a gesture which means he is inside.
Nayamika move forward, what she wants is to intelligible
her mind. This solo devotional trip is to reveal her to
herself.

How do you know about me?
As soon as the saint opened his eyes he asked in a faint voice.
I ..I have read about you.
Ok.So are you a follower of Rushikanth?
Yeah .. I loved his thoughts.
Yeah. Why you are here, Nayamika?
Why you are asking me, you can predict the future, right?
I can read the thoughts with the help of person In front of me.
Yeah.
But you are not cooperating.
No, I am allowing you to read my mind
But I can't
Why?
Because you have covered your real thoughts with something
else,like your masking your real destination by yourself.
Me? No .
Yes, Nayamika, first avoid the inessential thoughts, then your
destiny will be visible for you.
How?

Find those irrelevant past memories that struggles you and solve it like a warrior. Find it, then burn it. If your missing someone or something just find it and ask yourself, if it is with you now, then will it create a permanent satisfaction for you?

I ? I don't know.

No Nayamika, once you find it, then you will find your real happiness. What was God Krishna's life destiny? Will he be happy even if he spends all his time on Vrindhavan, with Radha? never? He knows his destiny move to Madurai.

So?

You have to unearth it.

There was a silent spreads over there.

Then you can leave here, because I can't help you, only you can help you.

She walked with a bare mind, she didn't understand why everyone is talking like this, no one is saying clearly, here everyone is talking in an impenetrable way.

Nayamika again walked through the snow-covered narrow path, near to a small spring with primula flowers bloomed on its banks.

Himalayas are the serine land of our earth. Every where is surrounded by rich, sunny yellow primula flowers trimmed with silver farina around the base, filling the air with their heavenly honey perfume.

I am feeling more relaxation here.

But why Everyone is asking me the same question, why you are here?

I am also wants to know why God has given an opportunity for me to born on earth. Why I am here on the earth.

She tries to console her mind from the distracting thoughts and close her eyes and look at the great Himalayas to get the answer as well as question

What struggles me more? What is the cause of my grievance?

Is that the feeling of no body to depend upon?

From which day I feel I am alone?

Am I alone in this world?

From my birth? or before that?

Did I hear anything wrong related to me during the time in my mother's womb?

Why?

Why?

Everyone asked me why I planned a solo trip to Himalaya.
I don't know but I want to get a relief from my past wounds.
when I am in a trouble, suddenly I will fall into the past whirlpool of wounds and that will swish me apart.
That makes me to go below the line and totally losing everything.
After suffering some preliminary depression zones, I realized, I cant manage my soul by myself. And after my depression stage, it may not be a depression that defined in psychology, but I am calling it as depression, I never consult any psychologists for that I myself come out from it, But then I feel a loneliness, an isolation , an urge of escaping from every one.
So we Indians believe the positivity coming from our north, hence I am here. I found an answer for the question why I am in Himalayas.

3

A Probe to
Childhood Memories

When she starts thinking about herself, she is viewing everything like a movie and every single thing strikes her mind.Is that because of the holy land?

When Nayamika was about 4 years old, she was studied in a nursery school near to her home.She love her father to come and escort her back to home. That day she waited for her father for a long time in the verandah of the yellow painted nursery building and finally her teacher closes the gate and she said she will bring me back to home, at that time her chacha came running and little Nayamika feel happy when she saw her loving chacha.

Chacha is her father's younger brother and he loved her like his own kid.

Chacha… are you came here to bring me back to home?

Yes. Sweetie.

He walked towards my teacher and say something in a murmuring voice.

I didn't understand what did they speak as I am in the extreme happiness.

Chacha took me and Anointed over his bike and take my bag and hold it in the handle. I feel I was ordained as a queen.

When he starts the bike, I said

Chacha , papa is coming in bicycle and he is moving slow but the bike is moving fast. Then we can move in the same

speed of bycycle . He agreed imitates the sound of bike and I laughed loudly.
Chacha , where is pappa? he will buy milk ice from here.
I pointed to a small Ice cream shop in the opposite side of the road.
He pretends to be happy when he heard that.
He stopped at the same shop and bought milk ice but he was in a rush so I planned to keep it at my hand and eat it when I reach home as I found he is moving with a speed and I afraid whether my milk ice will slip down from my hand.
When we reach home, I jumped from the bike in order to show my happens. I feel mamma is not in a happy mood and she shows her anger in her face.
Grandpa, Grandma, everyone stood near me and grand pa moved his hands over my hair.
Grandma bring some tea and I refused it and start licking my milk ice.
Mamma, where is pappa, he likes milk ice and I want to give it to him for liking it once.
I was not in an age to understand the anger and tears in mamma's eyes.
She raised with a violent tone and I didn't completely understand what she said, but I get the point that pappa went somewhere and will not come back. Grand pa and Grand ma tried to console her.
He left us.
He left me.
He leaves his sweetie and run away.
Is it?
I didn't believe, how can he leaves me
He asked me to give thousand kisses in today morning and I have given uncountable number of kisses to him. Will his eyes got wet at the time?
Why he didn't bring me to the place where he went?
While I am listening to everyone, milk ice fell down, on the floor. When I try to take it back, Chacha showed a gesture not to take it.
Grand pa will you ask pappa to bring me a milk ice when he returns?
I asked in a low voice.
But Mamma heard that.
oh god how i will make her understand that her pappa wont come back, why god is this much cruel to my girl.
I hate the god when I heard that. Why god is so cruel to me.

I moved slowly to our room where we sleep together.
There I got the smell my father.
I move closer to the area where he usually slept. I feel a warmth
there. A drop of tears rolled into my cheeks.
After sometime chacha entered to the room, I was laying
on my father's space on the bed.
He asked, sweetie , do you want tea and biscuits?
I nodded my head, by refusing it.
He sat near me and dip the Parle g biscuits in hot tea carefully
without dropping down
What happened to pappa? I asked in a low voice
Sweetie, he went for a trip.
A trip? without me, to a park?
No sweetie, it is not a trip to a park. He went to visit temples.
And one day he will come back.
Tomorrow?
May be after some tomorrows.
Then I won't talk to him, he left without me.
He smiled and hugged her.
Yes sweetie. One day he will surprise you. Then we can beat him
like this. He mocked like he was doing a Rustling with me.
I feel agreeable at that moment I swept the mucus from my nose
because of crying and smiling at the same time.
One day he will come back. I started waiting for that tomorrow
 to come.
Whenever i am sitting alone, I start thinking about my Pappa. I felt
that if he is with me, I will be happy and whatever struggles me
will get vanished when I lean in to his shoulders.
I miss him badly. If anything hurts me, all my past wounds start
stabbing me inside, and i cant handle the situation like everyone
else is doing.

4
Decision to Become Studious

Gradually everything has changed. Mamma became more strong and started a job at the pickle factory near to our house and she became financially independent. Chacha is buying the school accessories for me and gifted everything with extreme love .

Frequency of asking the question of when pappa will come has reduced.

But when ever I did a small mistake, mamma lose her temper and compare me with the abandoned dad.

When I am in third standard and I got 01/10 for an English dictation.

Actually forgot about it and didn't study any word. Teacher didn't scold me as she knows I have got score 8 or 9 in the previous dictations.

While hand overing the answer sheet she asked with a sweet voice.

Why Nayamika, have you forgot about the dictation?

I shook my head and eyes got wet.

No need to worry my darling, study for tomorrow's test and must score full marks. Cheer up my girl. She patted on my back.

I expect the same from my mother so I showed that answer sheet to her, even an option of hiding and lying was there.

As soon as she saw it she yelled tear that page and shouted at me.

Ey baboon, You are exactly like your father, he spoiled my life and now you also doing the same. Is it a gift for me from my kid in order to make me happy? You have no idea about how much I am struggling now. I didn't live a moment for myself. Everything is my fate. I am a cursed women and will burn myself soon and show you. And you are also maledict.

She continued by taking a deep sigh.

Its my fate. But I want you never suffer like I did. You must have knowledge, a secure job then only you have a value in family as well as society. If your husband leaves you, or who ever left you doesn't pull you into a miserable situation. You need not struggle like am doing now. You cant imagine how much your mother is suffering from society as well as from family. I don't know why your father left us and I am by effecting all those things. why God has given such a miserable life to me.

I stay red handed in front of her. I didn't get marks. I didn't study for the particular test. I did an aberration it must be correct.

I was only 10 years at that time and didn't understand why she scolded me that much. It was only a class test not any important exam.But then I promised myself that I never forget to study.

Yet I keep my promise.I studied hard, not for me but for my mamma's happiness.

5

Enjoying Chacha's Love

Soon after chacha becomes my best friend and everyday he visits us and play with me.Chacha buys sweets for me, chacha came to bring me back to home from school. He tried to behave like my pappa.

When I was sleeping in a Christmas vacation, and suddenly identified chacha's sound and ran to varandhah.

mamma makes me stop by holding my hands tightly.

Go inside miku!

I got terrified and panicked by hearing her loud voice.

With the shivering lips I asked in a low voice,

Can I talk to chacha?

At the same moment without or with hearing that chacha spoke loudly.

I cant let you to give all the properties of my brother because if he come back on one day I want to give everything back to him.

So..what I want to do brother? Can I kill this kid and suicide? Is that what you need.

She spokes with a shivering sound and I feel just now her eyes will burst.

I was hearing my mamma's loud voice only after pappa's disappearance. Before that she was quite happy and here face was calm.

I looked at chacha and showed a smiling face to him. But he didn't
give attention to me.
This is why my brother left you.
Chacha said it like a statement in a murmuring voice. Then
mamma become very angry and behave like she has some
mental issues.
She yelled ,cried , scold and I was just a kid who didn't
understand what all things are happening around me.
Finally, when chacha didn't mind anything and asked us to
evacuate the house she wept her tears and pack
everything and come out, by holding my hands tightly.
She yelled at me.
come fast Nayamika , those devils want us to leave here.
Everyone looked at us and no one came there to help us.
I bring my school bag and accessories with me.
Mamma hire an auto and ask me to get in.
I want to look at chacha. Why he is doing like this? What
happened to him.
But I am not brave enough to look at him.
I stood my head and obey what mamma said.
We reach in front of an old, small house and mamma went out
like a warrior and said:
From today onwards, we will stay here.
I have thousands of questions to ask. But didn't ask anything.
Then gradually from my mother's words I understood chacha
didn't loves me.If he do so, he will not let me to leave
that house.
I really loved my new house, always I tried to love what I have
at present.
But chacha influenced me a lot and that I understood later. In
every evening at school, I expect chacha to come and hug
me and bring me to our old house. If a bike passes near to
our house, I automated peep through the window to check
whether chacha was coming or not.
Nothing happened. I never saw him again.
But my poor mind isn't accepting that for a long time.

6

Getting Appreciation
from School

Years go on.. when I am on my eight th standard and I am studying well and I am ranked to 4 out of 25 among the pupil of my class. I was good in science and weak in mathematics. After a terminal examination the answer answer sheets are distributed by a new teacher, Druv, he was very young and handsome.

I have scored the maximum marks for physics and he declare physics is his favorite subject. When I feel a brotherly bond with him everyone else in my school feel a crush on him.

I liked his vibrant smile and low pitch sound and he has a very thick black hair and a well-managed moustache.

Soon he became the allure of our school. As he was friendly in class, he became our favorite teacher. By the effect, everyone starts studying physics and for me it leads to a competition. Everyone aimed to score better than me in physics but for me it was a prestigious issue. Anyway, that makes me a master in physics. Every time when sir asked me to do a problem on board, I feel I am on the top of the world and in my mind, he become my elder brother to support me, guide me and care me. I believed that he was my brother in my past birth.

I feel that he is also caring me and constantly asking me to find a dream and go for it.

Basically I am not brilliant but I work hard. I like biology more than physics but sir's appreciation was a prestigious issue, so I behaved that I like physics more than any other subject.

At that time our school conducted a space camp and which was led by Druv sir and it was a night camp.

I entreated my mother to join the one-day camp and she strongly refused. I feel a pain. But I don't want to insist her. So, I painfully accepted, her decision.

On the next day when Druv sir came to note the name of student's participating in the camp while going through the sheet, he suddently raised his head in search of me. That moment I tried to hide from him so adjust my position at the exact back of the student Infront of me.

By holding the sheets on the hand, he come near to me and looked to my eyes.

I was searching for a better lie for an explanation.

He didn't ask anything and left the classroom. Afternoon there were no classes and everyone is excited about the sky view camp at night. I lay down on the table by holding by backpack. I have no strength to insist my mother, actually I am not afraid of my mother but I don't want to force anyone. If she understand it herself and allow me to join the camp, it will be congenial.

That evening when I reach home, mamma was waiting for me with a cup of tea. I flashed a voltage less smile to her and she said go for a bath and get ready to the skyview camp.

I was totally excited. Really??

Why mamma, why you let me to go?

Because Druv sir contacted me and so…

Really, Did sir called you, over phone?

She groaned.

I was super excited and I change my dress three times inorder to find the perfect match for the night camp.

Finally I have found out my favorite white salwar.

I was only 15 years but at that time everyone is wearing salwar with pinned dupatta and behaved like a thirty year old women.

Mamma accompanied with me and when we reached there by a rickshaw I feel it is a spectacular moment in my life.

Druv sir was arranging telescopes and he was very busy but I want to see him and want to convey my regards.

With in fifteen minutes every parent left and there were only dim lights in that school compound.

It was a first experience for me to enjoy night. Usually at 7 o clock mamma will close all the door and windows and I am not supposed to go outside after that.

Suresh babu, a professor from IISc inaugurated the camp and he explained about the universe and I was very curious to know about it more. I noted each and every point in my diary.

Then using a projecter we have seen a presentation about the astrophysics mainly about blackholes.

Finally at the end our headmaster praised Druv sir for giving the students a chance to know about the universe and thanked him for his hard work. We all clapped or hands in a rhythm.

In the middle of heavy applause he ran to ground for focusing one star.

We followed him and others teachers asked as to arrange in a queue.

One by one is watching the sky and finally it was my turn.

When I reached near to Druv sir with his ever sunning smile he welcomed me.

Nayamika, are you able to see the brightest object in the sky, it was Sirius and it is 8.6 light years away from us. and so..

After the skywatching everyone is leaving from ground, sir call out my name from back.

Nayamika, come here

I ran to him

If you have any doubts you can clear it with suresh babu sir. Come with me

Actually I have no doubts and I feel emptiness in my head. But I followed him.

When I reached near to professor suresh babu, I have no idea about what to ask

But Druv sir introduced me by saying

Sir, this is Nayamika who is the topper in our school and want to join iisc after completing her plus two studies.

I was totally wondered. I never have a dream like that and I thankful to him for choosing a dream for me.

Professor give me the ways to join IISc and sir enthusiastically listen everything and I stood behind him

At the moment I feel that I want to hug him like I did with my father and he should pat on my shoulders.

That night I can't sleep. I got a dream, I got a destination.

I never worry about my father or chacha,

Never feel embarrassed because of mamma's words or her behaviour.

I start studying more in order to get more love and care from
        my teachers, especially Druv sir.
They loved me and I feel elevated at every second in school.
I feel that these teachers will be with me for my entire life.
Druv sir will guides me, through out my life
But that was also my distant wish.

After final exams I never went to school until the results get
        announced.
That day was the happiest day for me and I got 87% and become
        the topper in school.
When I reach the school in the afternoon, I saw Druv sir was
        talking over mobile and I smiled at him.
I expected a very powerful and charming smile but he just
        flashed a smile on me.
Every one including headmaster appreciated me at the
        staffroom then sir came, without giving me a hand of
        appreciation, he said
You shuffled during the time of study vacation that's why not
        scoring more than this.
I feel that he strongly thrashes on my cheeks
My face got paled.
I feel that I will cry in front of all the teachers.
I want to ran to home.
soon my friends also came there,so I forced to stay there for more
        time. During our chating, someone said druv sir is going
        to get married. And he posted that on his facebook page.

I didn't get the connection. If he is going to get married , then why
he is not appreciating me, this isn't a good result?Feel a pain in
my left chest
I cried without reason.
Everyone appreciated me except sir. From whom I excepted an
appreciation.
I also lesson my score. This is not the best. You didn't work hard.
I made a decision after that.
Never ,,ever give anyone any ,space in mind.
I was only 15 at that time, I want to be childish but I wear a
        mature mask on my face and keep everyone in my head
        and block the passage to my mind.

7

Raising of New Nayamika

I was in my teenage but never wore any teenaged attire as I
feel love never shower on me in this attire.
Mamma want to admit me in the St Johns convent school where
I get entrance coaching during my higher secondary
education.
It is a well disciplined school and everyone from there surely
get an admission in top colleges.
But I have to stay there.
I didn't feel much sorrow about that. Because our home is also
like a hostel.
When I returned from home mamma wont be there. And when
she come back from the company I went to my area for
studying. Same routine,everyday
As I shifted to hostel, I feel a peacefulness in mamma's face.
But my eyes got wet without my concern.
The school and hostel are superstructural and I wonder how
mamma will afford all those fees here.
Everyone in my hostel room are rich, beautiful girls like a model
in beauty shows and trying get attracted and I walk in
the opposite direction side by cursing myself.
I don't have a father, no house, no money and not beautiful. I
hardly wore bindhi, or applying kajel on my eyes.
I was just a regular student in class who do every work on time.
Will go for entrance coaching on weekends on time and will do
problems.
Neither laugh loudly , nor mock anyone.

Only my new classmates are coming to me for the sake of getting my notebooks.

I shrink inside my own shell. I found peacefulness in that.

While my rich, gorgeous room mates getting ready for going to entrance coaching institute which is just 1 km away from hostel, I was doing problems in physics.

They put makeup, wear costly dresses and consider me as a scholarly pupil.

But I know I was not that much intellectual. Sometimes I score lesser than them. But this erudite behavior is a veil that hides me from doing everything that once I enjoyed in life.

They often went out for having food and shopping, the never asked me to accompany them because of this studious pupil veil. I always open any one book on my table and read it mindlessly so no one will approaches me for saying anything. My roommates also feel free that I am not participating in any of their activities.

I never go for their birthday parties, their outing and slowly they stop inviting me for their occasions. That was what I need. I have no money to spend with them, i can understand how much my mother is struggling to pay my monthly fees.

I never complained to mamma about not giving me pocket money as I know her monthly income.

The walls of my hostel may never hear my sound, my laugh, or my giggling. They may understand me from my thoughts. I am Also behaving like a non leaving thing like the wall near to my bed in hostel room.

I believed that no one in the school is noticing me until I saw my name scratched on the wooden table.

8
Knowing about
the secret lover

That was the time of plus one board exam and I was about to
complete the exam, tied my sheets and take it for ascertain.
That moment I saw something scratched on my table
It was written as nayamika in a cursive beautiful handwriting.
I got panicked suddenly. Will teacher think that it is me who
scratch my name on table? But this is not my handwriting,
mine is not cursive like this, so I can prove.
Soon after, a gentle breeze flows through my mind and I feel
someone in the school is loving me so much without my
concern.
That feeling create a cooling in my mind and it put off all the
heat in it.
I looked around.
Everyone is busy in answering in the last five minutes.
I feel cold as ice. Something sticked inside my throat.
I afraid to look around. I shook my head and ran to hostel .My
heart was shivering for a long time.
Then I console myself that it may be any other Nayamika, not
me.
But I am sure that there is no other Nayamika in my school.
Then? Who did that?
That day was the last day of plus one classes and I even didn't
say bye to anyone and ran away.
My heart become elated for the first moment in life it was
imaging a love story of mine with a handsome guy,

I tried hard to control the delighted thoughts of my mind by saying that I am not beautiful, I am not rich, I am not talkative, in order to make it little down.

But, that imagination of mind actually killing me in each and every second. When the phone rings, my mind will get alerted that it will be the person who secretly loves you.

When the postman arrives, it will say, oh he sends a lovely card for you.

Sometimes I reproach myself for thinking like this.

But I was on my sweet seventeen and my mind knows that better than me.

Still I have no courage to look around.

I have lost my sleep.

I have no besties to ask.

I have no close cousin to discuss.

Me and my mind made some love stories and somehow I started enjoying that.

I started watching love songs and there will be smile along with some other feeling came to my mind.

I used to put kajol in my eyes and comb my hair and two three times change the hair style.

I feel that something sparkling in my eyes.

I noticed that I become more attractive.

I sensed that I start repeating love songs in my mind.

First time in my life, I want to put nail polish in my nails.

I want to wore some fancy jhmukkas to get more attraction.

But I never tried.I start loving myself.On that two week vacation at home I tried some home remedies to get attracted, I put buttermilk on my face along with turmeric but the color of turmeric wont disappear. Evening when mamma returns from job she groaned at me by seeing the yellowish color.

9

He is Giving More Hints

When the time to declare the results of the plus one exam I feel tensed. I can't share my tension with my mamma, I don't know why. She was also busy with her works and never tried to console me.

At least I expect she will come and tell me don't worry you will get good marks and come to have food.

At the night,

I cant sleep.

I cant concentrate.

I am totally spend the day before the commencement of the result in a panicked state.

I got some relief when I think about the person who loves me.

In a hypnagogic state, I feel someone is sitting near to me and curdling me by moving their hands over my hair.

I feel I am hearing a sound

Don't get panic, none of your results will desire your destiny. And also, you will get good score than ever. be happy.

I tried to imagine the person. But I found I have no supernatural

powers but still I feel my mind knows the person and it hides his face from me. Even I don't know him still I start loving him.

I fell into sleep peacefully.

In the morning I went to café for getting my results. There was a huge crowd in the café and café owner said kartwork is slow so you have to wait. I have waited on the chair placed outside. I closed my eyes in order to pray. My hands are shivering due to tension as well as hunger. Some of them

went to the nearby computer centers but I feel a fizziness
over my body so I decided to return home.
When I near to my home I saw mamma is talking with some
of neighbors and she looks excited.
Why she isn't thinking about my results? No tension at all.
I feel embarrassed.
While I am removing the sandals she looked at me with an
intense happiness and declare,
I was sure that you will get it.
What mamma?
I didn't get the connection.
Are you trying to mock me?
No, what mamma. Do you get my score?
Yeah. Just now one of your school mate called in our landline
and you secured 91% dear.
I didn't hear all the words.
I feel happy to get 91 percentage.
Mamma whom called you, Nithya?
No miku, that is a boy and he said his name, I forgot,it was a
strange name.
She turned back to kitchen while my neighbors congratulating
me. Soon she returns and said
Is there any Piyush in your school? I think that was his name.
There is a Piyush in our school and who was our school leader
and everyone knows him. I too have seen him.
Why he contacted me?
From where he get my phone number?
How he knows my score?
Is that correct? My score?
A thousand questions came to my mind and none I can answer.
I got 91% that was not an astonishing news for me as I worked
hard.
But why Piyush called me?
Did he call every one of my class?
To get the answer I called my bench mate Nithya.
Nithya, this is Nayamika. Do you get the score card?
No Nayan. And congratulations, hope you are happy.
Yes Nithya.thank you. How do you know about your score?
Nayan, we were there in the café in the morning I saw you. But
I am inside it and because of the crowd I cant come to
meet you.and there was some network problem so we
went to town.
Ok, Nithya.

How do you get your result?
I..I didn't get it from café at that time but I get to know it.
I told a lie.
I cut the call. I want ask Nithya that Piyush was also there or
      not.
If he was there, its natural that to check the top scorer of school.
Is it Piyush who written my name on the table?
No.never.that won't happen.
He is handsome, mature and very smart.He is teacher's idol. I

have seen that he was talking to teachers in the staffroom in a
very friendly manner.I have noticed that he was mocking
with the mathematics teacher.I have noticed that
our Hindi miss is always walking through the
verandah by talking to him.Mostly he was inside the
staffroom or in the surroundings during the interval or
lunch break.

Everyone in my class may have crush on him. So, I erased the
connected dot.

Piyush surely not the person whom I am searching. May
our principal informed him to call and announce the marks
of the students who was not at the hostel now. I
tried to believe.
But my imaginative, mind start sculpting a new rhythm for
my body at its sweet seventeen.

10
The urge of getting loved

From the shell of insecurity, I came out to a world of love. Every day I feel that someone is loving me. That gives me some sort of strength.

After the vacation, I was too excited to go to school.

While I am walking towards the school gate, my body was shivering.

I was an early coming student in the school. My mind announced that someone is waiting for me with a flower. I didn't see any one else there. I turned around.

No. it still lying.

I reached my place and sat on the chair. To dream more, I lay down on the table. All of a sudden, I saw a flower on the

> drawer of my table.It was newly harvested with some water droplets.I want to take the flower but my hands are trembling

No one is there.

I looked through the windows and found that some of my classmates are coming.

With a strange impact I took the flower and join my hands and bring it close to my heart.
Then suddenly with the urge of hiding I put it inside my backpack.
I feel my hands are burning.
I feel I have hidden an atom bomb in my bag.
I didn't want to show that to anyone. Still, I have no courage to

look at any eyes of the boys in my class and to find who is loving me. I only have some familiar faces in my class who is asking homework's for copying, others are still strangers for me. I tried to become an introvert during the last two years. I am sitting on the first bench of my classroom and never turn back to see others. And the school is also not giving any practices to mingle the students.

I have heard from my bench mates that the mathematics teacher got angry when she saw some girls are sitting beside boys and our class is just near by the staffroom so during the interval times also we are under the surveillances of teachers. I want to find the person but I have no close friend to ask.

I am completely sunken in the love of an unknown person. Because I feel no one in this world is loving me.

I am sure that if the person loving me must be genuine because in my class as well as school so many pretty girls are there and they are friendly too. I didn't apply talcum powder or any cosmetics on my face still that day when I see my name on the table in examination hall. I want to talk and want to be friendly with others but never tried to do it.

Who loves this typical girl?
After that when I am walking through the verandah, I hear some pampering noices.
Go and tell her,
Oh,, she is coming..
Go and talk to her..
Why you are hesitating..
If I turnback I can find the person.
But I am not daring enough.
Slowly I realize everyone except me knows about my lover.

11
He Starts Caring

I want to study, nonetheless I want to think about my love.
I never think that I will fall in love with an unknown person in
my life, as I didn't show any love to anybody in the last
couple of years, that is integrated and become a large
quantity of love. I am keeping this love and it is almost
ready to burst out.
I heard from every one that we won't get any time for sleeping
during these two years as we have a lot of things to study.
But I feel I am unoccupied during these days.
Everyone in my hostel room is looking at me with a strange smile.
I was delightful.
One Sunday, after entrance coaching, when we come out from
the institution by searching for my umbrella in my bag
pack as it was raining outside.
My room mates are staying at verandah, as they didnt bring
their umbrella. I have my umbrella I asked Nithya to come
with me.
I can accommodate one more person inside my umbrella.
But everyone shows a hesitation to come, they reap the benefits
of rain by talking and sharing their friendship.
I too want to stay there.but my bookish nature illicit me from
staying there.
I opened my umbrella and walk unescorted to cross the road.
There was a heavy rush in the zebra cross and I just reach the
middle of road, devastating wind blows and at the same
moment ,my umbrella bend in the opposite direction.

I cursed myself that I am using same umbrella for more than
five years and it lost its stability to stay stationary during
the wind.
I cant wait there to make it proper, it was raining heavily and
so many other persons are crossing the road. Someone
moved their umbrella from my back and I leaned in to it
and mine I just carry like a stick.
When I reach the opposite end of the road,I turned around
to say thanks to the person.
Though the person whom offers me a space in the umbrella,
move away by giving me a side face.
Blood rushes to my heart.
Is that Piyush??
Yes.it is.
He gives me a side face.
I am blushed with love.
I was not bravery enough to look around.
I feel everyone in our institute is looking at me.
I didn't look at anyone after the moment as I guess there was a
smile on my face and that was involuntary.I feel my heart
was dancing with joy as I can hear a rhythm inside
my body that overcomes the sound of rain.I closed and
opened my eyes at a greater speed and rubbed my foot
together.
I didn't sleep at night. My heart bear out that Piyush is the
person who loves you.
Nevertheless, my brain says it's not him.
And brain proved that with some evidences.
He is smart,handsome and most of the girls have crush on him.
I never talked to him.
I never smiled at him.
I never look into his eyes.
Can such a person love this girl?
Never.
He is not loving you.
And nobody will fall in love with you.
I scratched my wounds caused from love.
My pappa, chacha, druv sir.
love depends on beauty,money, social status.
He is the top scorer in every mock exam and he want to become
a doctor.
Me, just showing that I am a bookish intending to get away from
people.

Not brilliant girl.
Just hardworking.
I don't want to hurt me again.
I shrink back to my own space.
Nayamika,don't go for love. It will hurt you.He will leave
you   unnoticed like your pappa, chacha,sir..
Sweetie……
I feel I have heard my pappa's voice.
I lay down on my bed, tears rushed into my cheeks.
I cried and try to take out the part of my mind has some love
        towards an unknown person.
It was bleeding, my I scolded my mind to create such a love.
Everything may be your hallucination.
You imagined that there was a handsome boy who loves you.
I passed a weak smile.
Yeah, correct. It may be my imagination.

12

Desire for Mother's Care

I forcefully controlled me as I have no one to discuss about this and get an opinion.Nextday,I didn't put bhindi, I haven't look at the mirror, went to school. When I reach the school gate, I can see a group of students stay there and they make some noise when I reach near to them.

I just move away without looking anyone but didn't bow my head.

Instantly the noise come to an end.

Did he read my eyes?

So, he shows some gestures to his friends to stop making noise?

All of a sudden, the love hormone starts working.

I just tried to control it. But when the moment I lose the track of controlling it, it blows with all its strength.

There was a debate inside my mind about Piyush, I can't concentrate on lectures, and as I feel he was walking outside my class room, I turned my eyes in that direction.

I nodded my head as soon as I saw him.

Yes, he was walking through the veranda.

Suddently,our English teacher Priya, noticed my movements and she called out my name.

Nayamika, what happened?

I..I.sorry ma'am. I stood up and say slowly.

Everyone looked at me and I sat like I am humiliated.Tears filled in my eyes and I controlled it to not to burst out.I took a deep breath and control my mind.Eventhough I feel that I am killing my happiness, cheerfulness by not to think about him. I feel my head is paining and it will burst out soon. I want to change the surroundings.

In the afternoon I feel headache and went to home in order to control my thoughts and to avoid the meetings with him. That was first time in my life as I leaving school before the actual time.

When I reach the bus stop near to our house, not ours, rented one, I feel free in the first time in life. I want to meet mamma, I want to lay down on her lap like a kid. And want to get a head massage from her.

When I changed my character, after so many rejections from childhood, I didn't show my real character in home too. I didn't show my love towards mamma and she also never fondle me. Now, I feel the need my mamma's love.

In the huge urge of talking to mamma, I walked fast to reach home.

Now I can see her head; she was talking to someone.

Oh, its Madhu uncle. I have identified him from a nearer view.

As soon as I reached near to them, I feel that they are arguing about something and meanwhile mamma noticed my presence, I saw her anger turned into affection.

Miku, why you are here now.? All your exams over, why not informing me?

Nothing ma, just a two-day study vacation.

Hi Madhu uncle,

I greeted him.

Hi Miku. I can see a mixed feelings in his face.

He smiled at me and greeted as soon as he left there.

Mamma, what happened to him.

Every one's real character revealed at some moment of time dear.

Eh? Mamma is also become philosophical.

I laughed.

Actually I am taking her like this after so many months, I just inform her my examination dates, fee, and results, for the past months I have nothing to tell more than that.

She was also relieved by my presence. She make my favorite dish ela ada by adding more jaggery and coconut scrapes . I walk through the yard and carefully cut banana leaves and help mamma to make ela ada.

In the evening I enjoyed it with hot tea in front of my television watching my favorite film thirakkada.

How intense is love.

Soon I realized, my mind may mislead me by seeing love movies, so I changed the channel. Then I heard a calling bell;

mamma went outside to open it.I can identify the sound of Madhu uncle, I didn't listen what they spoke. Within fifteen minutes there conversation becomes argument and I can hear my mamma's voice as she is saying Miku was inside and he should keep quiet.
But he wasn't lower his voice, so I went outside.
His appearance shows that he was drunken and messy.
I just peep through the door, and went back to kitchen for taking one more elaada.
I was about take it, while I heard a panic uttering of my Mamma,
Somebody please come,help..help
It was dropped from my hand, neglecting that,I ran to veranda.
Madhu uncle fall down in the yard in front of veranda and blood was flowing from his head.
I looked at mamma, she was panicked and didn't look at me.
There were no people in the neighboring houses as there was some program in the nearby temple.Due to noice from the temple, her sound was evaporated in the air.I went out and saw a rickshaw is approaching and ask him for help.Me and mamma together try to made him to reach inside the rickshaw, but mamma didn't look at my eyes.
When the rickshaw starts moving, my eyes got wet.
I went back to the veranda and sat on my father's chair.
He usually sat on the chair and I too love to spend time by simply sitting on the chair.
Whenever I sat there, I feel a warmth.
I remember when Pappa and his sweetie together sat on the chair and Pappa with his hairy hand hugged me tightly. And the girl utters,
Pappa, more ..more..
A tear arises and get ready to fell down.
Again, I feel that I am alone in this world.
All the negative thoughts rushed to my mind.
My father left me at the time I need care.
I have no siblings to love.
I have no friends to share my situation.
No relatives to consoled me.
Mother is also not here when I need her presence.
No …
No.. lover to get love.
I got mad,by hearing noises from the temple, using my thumb I closed my ears.

That time my mind was also making noises that I am not able to
understand properly.
She moved her hands over her face in order to get some
relaxation.
Closed her eyes, she has no idea how much time she slept,until
the sound of bike received by her ears.
She opened her eyes, it was totally dark, she didn't put the
veranda light and sandhayadeepam so she couldn't
identify the person who came on bike.
In a hurry she switched on the light.
Two persons are in the bike and by the time one person get down
and walk towards her by showing some gestures to the
other one in the bike.
The second person left there and the face of the person who came
is now visible for me.

13

Piyush Reveals
His Love

Flabbergasted by his presence she stays quiet.
It was Piyush.
Still, she can't believe the things happened around her.
Piyush without her permission or invitation get into the
veranda, and sit opposite to her.
Nayamika, can I get some water?
She come back to reality. She nodded her head and moved
to kitchen.
She has given the glass of water and thousand questions
reflected in her face.
By reading his eyes, Piyush asked in a gentle voice.
You are going to ask, why am here, isn't it?
No, I nodded by telling a lie.
Then?
She shook her head as she is not getting any words.
She looked at his eyes.
Nayamika, don't you know that I am following you from the
last few years?
She again shook her head; she has no courage to look into his
eyes.
Are you fine, Nayamika, if I am sitting here until your
mother comes? Do you have any problem?
She feels that her heart will break soon, as she feels it pulses
more than the natural rate.

I don't know.

Finally, she spokes.

What you don't know? You mean the time when your mother arrives?That doesn't matter.

He is saying the question and answer by himself.

She has no idea about what to say to him, her eyes wandering through the tiny sand particles on the floor.She has perplexed by her thoughts and it was clueless to recollect.She feels she forgot to speak.

He smiled magically while looking at her face.

Nayamika,?

Yes. I again looked in to his eyes.

Are you comfortable if I am sitting here?

Eh? I nodded again to show yes.

There was tiny wonderful rain start showering at that time and she looked at that not to enjoy its beauty but to get rid of looking at him.

Its beautiful, right Nayamika. Its difficult to call your name again and again as it is lengthy but I am enjoying while saying it. She smiled.

Can I call you as Nayan.?

I again nodded.

Why you are so quiet,

I smiled and didn't give the answer.

Then I will say about myself.

I am Piyush Prabhakar, Prabhakar my dad is a doctor, specialized in gynecology and worked at KIMS Trissur, my mom shubha Prabhakar is a lawyer and I have an younger sibling, Prithvi Prabhakar studying in fourth standard. we have settled in Trissur, near vaniyamkavu temple, our house name is also Shubha, my mom's name.

I heard everything without blinking my eyes.I recorded everything in my memory.

And I know everything about you, N ayan. I collected every single bit of data about you.

He laughed after saying that.

She just smiled.

As she doesn't know how much time they sat opposite to each other without speaking any word, then her mother came.

Piyush stood up and greet mamma.

Mamma, I am Piyush, Nayamika's school mate. My aunt's house is nearby and when I found Nayamaika is alone here, I wait with her for your arrival.

I got completely impressed by his behavior.

How smart he is.
I smiled with pride.
Thankyou Piyush. Oh, you are the one who called and inform me the score of miku, last year, right? God bless you boy. I was totally disturbed when I was at the hospital as miku is left stranded here. And sorry for troubling you.
No, aunty, its my pleaure. I am leaving, aunt will be waiting for me.bye aunty, bye Nayan.
I smiled and let him leave. I try to hide the love shyness to mamma.
I went to my room and looked at the mirror.
Soon I feel embarrassed.
I didn't see a beautiful girl like a model on the mirror.
Is this Nayan? Whom he called with affection.
I looked at my last month's pimple marks on my oily face and fizzy hair that stand straight over head.
I took a comb and correct the hair, but still, it is misbehaving. I lose the confidence, how he looked at my face the last few hours.
I turned around, the veranda where he sat has so many scratches and the last paining is more visible than the present paining on the wall.
The chair was dirty and the front yard was totally covered with dry leaves shows that it wasn't cleaned.
I feel red faced.
Why he came here to make me ashamed? Everyone in school may get to know about the deteriorated house of their classmate.I don't want to go back to school.I know, Piyush is just feeling empathy on me and I don't want that.He knows everything about me so he has some commiseration towards me.I actually didn't want any sympathy or empathy. My thoughts become wired.
That day I hate my life and want to end my life.
Then another thought strikes in my mind.

14
Realizing the Depth of his Love

Why piyush didn't ask me about the incident? Did he think that there is an adultery relation between Mamma and Madhu uncle?

If I can explain to him, I will feel relaxed.

And I want to ask him, how does he know everything about me. Why he is following me?

I don't like someone is loving me intensively like this.

Something struck in my throat.

Who told me that he loves me???

A sudden reply arises in my mind.

I got panicked.yeah, he didn't say that he loves me. May he consider me as his sister and he will have a beautiful, rich girlfriend.

My thoughts got perplexed and I feel I am mad.I can't concentrate in my studies. Then,I promise myself that I never think about him till my exams get over.

Exams begins and I only reach the school just few minutes before the commencement of exams and ran to home when the final bell rings. I avoid the situations to meet him.

When I reached the school for the last examination, I was tensed a bit because I feel a total messy feeling over my head, though I didn't study carefully.Also,Last night electricity was out in our area that also affects my studies.That day I reached the school early in order to get a quick revision.

When I went out the bus, I automatically glanced at Piyush, who was reclined on a wall at the bus stop.I feel he was in some

dream and as soon as he saw me, he returned to reality.He walked towards me and further walks with me.
I didn't look at him.
Later, when we reach near to school compound, he spoke with a low voice.
Where were you for the last days? His voice was murmuring and I felt a sadness in it.
eh?
I raised a questioning look at him.
I am asking why you are avoiding me? He cleared the question by showing some sort of anger.
I didn't look at him , I looked at somewhere else.
I don't know. I replied with a faint voice to avoid him.
Do you know this is the last day of our school, and still, you don't want to talk to me?
He was saying like I am someone close to him.
I don't know.
Could you please look at me at least for the last time, I never trouble you after this?
It hurts me. I looked at him with a pain in my eyes.
Why you are behaving like you don't know anything?
I just nodded my head.
Oh, God, how can I convey to this girl.
He moved his fingers over the forehead.
He didn't complete the sentence but I want him to complete it.
He shows some impatience and he is behaving like he was some authority over me. There was a silence spread in between as and I feel he was tensed by my behavior.
I want to go.
I said as I noticed some of our teachers are coming. I was about to leave, he looked at my eyes and spoke with affection.
Nayamika,This is my number. Please call me when you are free.And, and I am leaving to Trissur today.
He gives me a piece of paper, there a mobile number is

beautifully written over it. I remembered the calligraphy on the desk which i found last year. He looked at my eyes and I feel he want to speak more. But that mutual gaze was enough for me. I feel a pain in my heart as he said he was leaving to Trissur. My eyes suddenly got wet and it begin to fell down. so, ran towards the class room.

When he says that he was about to leave from here, I feel he was trying take something from me and it was bleeding inside.

I don't remember whether I did the exam well or not, there was a song that streaming in my mind over the time.

When come out from examination hall, I noticed that Piyush was standing there with a bunch of boys.

I looked at him, he smiled at raised his eyebrows, asking why you are looking, I impulsively nodded my head showing nothing and he twinkled his eyes by closing his lips.He passed a mysterious smile and shows that he swept off my feet.I smiled with shy and shook my head.When I finally gaze a look at him, he closed his eyes and pat his chest, showing that he is with me.

I don't know how much I love the moment,

I was delighted, blushed with rejoice and I want to Frick at that moment.

If I get a chance to freeze my mind for the entire life, I will select this moment for my entire happiness.Still, I know I never be that much happy at any moment in the rest of my life.Still, when I am so weird and going through a perplexed state, I will recollect this moment to get a little relaxation. And it works.

15

Deep Rooting of Love

As soon as I reached home, I fell in to bed by reaching my pillow, I hold it tightly and bring close to my body.I didn't had food that day, I didn't wake up for dinner. All my sense organs were freezed by love.

I lay down on the bed by coloring my dream in the dark room. Piyush is holding my hands and we are walking over a misty hill station which is covered with snow. I moved closer to his body to feel warmer. He holds me tightly by his hands. There was a music played as background score. I lie down on his chest and he kissed on my forehead.

When mamma enters the room and switched on the light, I close my eyes and pretend to be sleeping.And continued my dream.He shows an affection to me in the way he looked at me.And why me, I wonder, as so many pretty girls are there in my school.

I crafted many questions for him, and during the day and night I was practicing those questions and expecting his answers. During my nap time, I recreated every moment with him.

May mamma noticed that I was dreaming all the day and didn't studying anything for coming entrance exam.

Miku, I didn't noticed that you are preparing for entrances, I don't have much money to send you to the top colleges, remember.

She said, when I was singing a Malayalam song

etho mazhayil nanavode namonnu kandu

theera mozhiyil mounangalaayalinju

eeran kaattil melle,maayum manjinte ullil

I didn't notice her arrival to my room where I sit usually for studying.
I feel it was a warning. I made so many objections but I
didn'tpresent it as I am not in an argument mood.I sit properly and open my book and start dreaming.I opened the piece of paper given by Piyush. I move my fingers through the numbers that written by him, I get electrified as I am touching Piyush with my fingertips. I smiled.
I want to contact him, but didn't get a chance. Mamma is always roaming around the living room there she kept the land phone.
Intentionally she asked about Piyush, two three times and somehow, I skipped the question, as I frighted that she will catch me red handed by my expressions and I am sure I can't control my happiness when I hear his name.
Day times I went to entrance classes and evenings mamma was there, so I never get a chance to call him.
One day, the day before the commencement of plus two results, I was little tensioned about the result and I come out from the coaching center and rejoiced by seeing Piyush at the bus stop.
Unintentionally I ran to him, why you are here?
With a shivering voice.
To see you.
Answer was crisp and quick.
I looked at him and blushed.
Why you didn't contact me.
I didn't get time.
Time? He asked by raising his eyebrows?
Not time, opportunity.
We both laughed together.
I forgot about the surrounding and stood closer to him.
Are you tensed about the results?

I don't know.
Oh, what is the need of a studious girl to think about her results.
No,no.not like that.
Then?
He is expecting something from me.
Nothing.
don't say like that. What you were thinking in this past 35 days.
Oh, it was 35 days.
Yeah. I counted day by day and struggling to stay there without
        seeing…
I control my shyness.
Seeing….
Seeing whom?
Whom?
He mocked me.
I laughed.
A few minutes later I found that most of our friends are looking
as with a dramatic manner, so I want to leave from there. I am
leaving.
Eh? Why?
Everyone is looking at us.
So,?
I am afraid.
For what?
They may misunderstand us?
Ha ha, misunderstand? It's not misunderstanding,its about
        understanding that we are in….
I smiled and looked around,
Keep quiet, everyone is listening.
Why you concerned about others, Nayan. You are mine,no
need to worry.
My tear buds opened and a drop of tear rolled at the corner of
my eye.
As he understands my uncomfortableness, he let me to go.
I moved forward, I don't want to leave, but there were many
familiar faces at the bus stop.
Must come tomorrow at school.
Piyush walked near to me and slowly said.
I looked at his eyes.
Don't want to go,eh?
No,no. I am going.
How long will you hide your love,Nayan?
I smiled.

16

The Proud Moment

I wake up early in the morning by little tensed about the result and more excited about Piyush.I wore a new salwar which I intended to wear when I met Piyush. It was of light green color , embroidered with pink flowers.

I am exhilarated that much to forget my admit card and realized that when I reach the bus stop.

No time to go back to home and collect it.

I have my mother's mobile,that mamma give today in order to call her and inform the result as soon as I get to know about it. I think about Piyush. I dialed his number and that was feed in my mind after so many times watching on the paper that given by Piyush.

Piyush attended the call.

As soon as she says hello, neurons passed the message through axons that it is your love.

Nayamika.Oh,nayan, from where you are calling?

Piyush,I missed my admit card, is that required to get the results.

No, Nayan. You come to school,I will collect a copy of your admit card from office.

Ok,is that fine?

Perfectly fine my girl.

If you have any problem, I will go back to home and bring it.

Oh, am I still a stranger for you? cheer up and come dear I will arrange it.

Thank you.
Eh? What did you say, I don't want a silly thank you.
Then?
That will say, later.Anything else Nayan, I am going to get ready.
Oh.ok.
Ok Nayan, I will there at the bus stop. waiting for see you. He cut the call.
She smiled.In the first time, she feels that she have someone to care.How fast he solved it. He cares me.Until today, I have no one to care me.Often my classmates discuss about their parents care, they help them to do an assignment, science project and get them their favorite things , their family get togethers, I get out from there to avoid unnecessary comparisons.My side was empty, no father, no relatives, only a struggling mamma.
Now I got a confidence. I met my man.I was in a trilling excitement.I feel reliance. I didn't stress myself about the results. Whether I get low or high scores, Piyush will be with me and will guide me.I take a deep breath and bury every bad experience in my life to a deep abyss.My eyes opened with confidence my lips curved to show it.
When I reach the school, I found that everyone looking at me with a strange feeling.
I saw from distance, Principal is smiling at me and shows me the gesture to come towards her.I turned by neck one eighty degrees to check, if there is any other person in my back, who was called by principal.She smiled and called me again, they I ran towards him. she patted my shoulder, and spoke.
Oh, you made me surprised Nayamika, I wonder how do you score 95 % in all subjects.
Other teachers are also reach towards me and I was blossomed with the congratulating messages.
Oh, Nayamika, the topper girl..
You are the proud of our school
Very good Nayamika, this is because of your hardwork.
Mathematics sir came and touched my head like blessing me and said, why you sat shy during the class time and I am really late to find a brilliant girl in my classroom.
I felt happiness for all the good words they shaver over me.I totally wonder, am I eligible for all these felicitations?My eyes instantaneously got wet and I say thanks to god for this beautiful moment. I feel blessed with their words

but,still my eyes searching for Piyush.Finally, when my
        eyes found him, he smiled at me with a magical graze.
I can't look at his eyes for a long time, I will get burnt with that
        feeling.
When everyone went for their own world, my legs automatically
        moved towards Piyush. While I reach near to him all of
        his friends scattered away by showing some gestures.
He smiled with adoration.
I realized the fond of love towards me.
Congratulations Nayan.
He gives a hand for congratulating.
I think about it for a while, his friends are watching, and may
        humiliate him, if I didn't give him hands.I touched the
        tip of his fingers and his fingers hugged them tightly and
        thumb patted on my finger's back.I have a heard the
        happiness of his friends by their wee sound.

I take my hands back.
We smiled and I found everyone else is gazing at us.
You go Nayan, he turned his eyes towards his friends by a feeling
that they might humiliate me.
He blinked his eyes
I smiled with love.
We didn't get much time to talk. But the eyes spoke everything.
so i returned to home.
 Mamma was happy and made some kheer for me.
But I expected she will come and hug me, or pat my back and
say, this is my girl.
But never happened.
Mamma don't know how to show love.Now I have no
        complaints about that.I tasted the kheer and watched
        television while I am thinking about Piyush.God please
        keep all these happiness with me or let me die today.
I have piyush, I got good score and everyone congratulated me.

I am the happiest person in the world. When the telephone rang,
and after a few minutes' mamma called my name Miku..
I ran towards the phone and catch the phone receiver.
With the palpitations, I said hello.
Nayan?
It was Piyush.I blessed. And hide my smile from mamma.
I am going back Nayan. Tomorrow morning pappa will come.
Oh, ok.
I feel a crack in my heart.
No need to stay here, school is over ,isn't it. He continued.

He mocked a quarrel tone.
Oh,
I know, for you it won't be a problem.but I can't..he sucked the
words.
Is there anyone near you.?
No.its fine.
Is that any problem to call you every day?
Eh? No
Can I call you every day?
Yeah.
Why just yes or no Nayan. I want to hear your voice,
I didn't speak much, as mamma can hear it.
What do you feel?
Eh? I don't know.
Will you please stop this, I don't know, I don't know. How far
        will you hide?
i..i didn't..
ok.then bye.
He cut the call.
I actually didn't expect that. There was something filled
from my stomach to heart.
Oh,hello..not able to here you. will call back.
I mocked infront of mamma as the call was disconnected
due to some other network issues.
I dialed his number that was quite familiar for me.
He picks the call on the first ring itself.
Oh, what is the matter?
He mocked a serious tone. I feel tensed. As he understand my
        silence .
Nayamika?
Eh, yes.
Nayamika..?
Tell me… I mocked his tone.
Nayamika, I am going back to Trissur by tomorrow morning,
        when I reach the home, it will be little difficult to call
        you.but I will manage.
Ok.
Can I cut the call as you are not saying anything?
Ok,bye.
Bye.
I feel sad. I want to continue the talk until my death.I was excited
        reach upto infinity.There was a silence filled in the air.
        The call wasn't disconnected.He spokes again.

Nayan, do you want to say anything.?
Mamma was there in background.
I just grumble.
is mamma there?
I murmured
Yes
Ok.good night dear.bye.
I want to talk to him so many things.but it wasn't possible infront
of mamma.I feel dejected.I missed a chance to be
happy.The night I was totally with Piyush and I thought
he may also feel my love.I want to ask him so many
questions.Why he likes me, that was the most important
one.

17
Sunken in Love

I was totally sunken in the ocean of love created by Piyush. I believed that I never fall in love. But I have experienced my change, the secure feeling I experienced, the care I possessed, the warm, comfortable feeling I experience now.

He called me at day times over telephone, so I asked mamma that I will continue my entrance studies by myself. Hence, I was free to attend the calls.

He said everything about his family. Though I expect he will ask about me also. I panicked that if he wants to know about my pappa, how I will control my tears infront of him. But he didn't ask anything about my family.He usually says about his brother with a love and I feel he considers him as his own kid. Routinely when we speek over phone, Prithvi will come and disturbs him. I silently hear the love and caring he has given to Prithvi.

I have no one to give care and to get care. I sometimes miss a sibling like Prithvi. And soon I will correct it, luckily God stops the arrival of my sibling to earth and he get escaped from everything.

Now I am living here only because of piyush,as my nerves are contracted by the arrival of continuous problems. Once Madhu uncle's wife, Preethi came our home and quarreled with my mamma, that was a new incident to get pressure in head,as she was thinking that he spends all his money to us. Also, she spoke violently and say some vulgar words on mamma. Mamma stood silently and she repeated the same sentence again and again.

No Preethi, I never borrow any single pai from madhu.

I feel it is genuine. Because I have seen her struggles for money.

I don't want to believe that my mamma is borrowing or cheating anyone to takecare of her father abandoned daughter. Everyone in our neighborhood peeped through their windows by opening it partially and enjoyed the scene. I feel I am sure that my mamma won't do any mistakes. May she has considered Madhu uncle as a brother or simply a person for supporting her. But the world believed that there should be some adultery relation between a middle-aged women deserted by her husband and a mature, rich man.

I didn't understand the type of their relation but I never asked mamma about that. I don't want to hear that Madhu uncle spends the money for us. I didn't asked Mamma about the incident happened on that night, how Madhu uncle fell down on the yard.

Whether I am not in a relation with piyush, I may create a scene by asking about that, and if I feel mamma was a suspect, it may lead to the decision for my suicide. but now I am relaxed, I am not caring about what others think about me, I am in a fairly world created by Piyush.

I am the fairy who is floating in air and aesthetically moving without any fear. There was only happiness and I cant think about the problems or miseries I experienced. The area of brain that causes, tension, depression, miseries, everything masked with my love. I feel I have drunken some vodka and it permanently affects my temporal lobe. like the chronic alcoholic who was not tensed a bit about his future or anything.

After the Preethi auntie's incident, I have found none of our neighbors are coming to our home , but mamma didn't care anything as she has experienced more than this.

But when I saw them, they showed an empathetic pale smile, which causes an omitting tendency on me.

18
A Killing Gossip

On the very next day, I was washing my clothes and I have heard phone is ringing, and that was a music which will play only when piyush calls.
Ab Tum Hi Ho
Zindagi Ab Tum Hi Ho
Chain Bhi, Mera Dard Bhi
Meri Aashiqui Ab Tum Hi Ho
I ran inside and my small toe just hit the leg of the table, but didn't care it and took the phone as fast as I can.There was no missed call notification on it and I found it was an auditory hallucination, and smiled myself.I return to washing area, by a mere chance I have heard the murmuring of two neighbors in our area.
I want to close my ears but they listen it and send to my brain.
My father left the house as he knows about the relation between mamma and madhu uncle!
I can't control either my tears or my thoughts. Soon my body become ice cold and I sat on the ground as I feel I fell down.
My brain continuously asking questions and that makes me mad.
is that the secret my mamma hides from me?
My brain cells connect the missing dots, when pappa get to know about the relation, he leaves us, then chacha knows he also behaved rude and the terms between mamma and uncle fails they quarreled.
No,no,no
In my mamma's behaviour I never saw that she is flirting with anyone.She is bold, brave, strong.So never.But if people are saying like this, may piyush will also get to know about that.
No..my heart pained.
I want to kill those neighbors. But may others also say like that.so, killing myself is better.
I looked at my left hand, moved the righthand fingers over that to find the best vein to cut. Soon I hear the ringtone of my phone.

19

In the World of
Love Created by Piyush

Ab Tum Hi Ho
Zindagi Ab Tum Hi Ho
Chain Bhi, Mera Dard Bhi
Meri Aashiqui Ab Tum Hi Ho

I didn't get up, as I feel it was my illusion.When it rings twice, with a sudden urge, I ran and get the phone.
Hello
Hello,Are you not well Nayan?
I didn't say anything except a hello, then how could someone can find the other person's mood.
With the closed nose, I said,
I am ok Piyush.
A silent tear dropped from my eyes.
No don't lie, my girl, I can understand your feeling as I have connected a chip in our mind, that send me signals that my girl is not happy.So I called you by closing the door by pushing my brother out.
He is trying to make the situation lighter.
Piyush, do you really love me?
I didn't realize that why I asked that question, which was not suitable for the current situation. A silent wind blows around me.
Nayamika…?
I am sure that he may get shocked because of the sudden question. As we didn't discuss anything related to our relation yet.

I grumbled.
What happen? Why you ask me like that? He asked in a soft melodious tone
I don't know.
My answer was crisp.
Nayamika, are you serious?
I murmured, yes.
But, we didn't discuss about our relation yet.
Yeah.
I feel I have committed a mistake. No need to ask this in a hurry.
 Ok. We can discuss,not now.Prithvi is here.
He didn't cut the call.But I did.
I feel a little bit relaxed about the incident created by neighbors.But a little tensed about my question asked to Piyush.
But I am sure he loves me. He said it in different ways. I just asked it directly, only that much. I try to console myself. Any way we have to discuss about that, so it wasn't a problem for asking the person whom you love.I waited for his call until mamma came.
I want to ask to mamma, but I feel if I ask, I will become an unfaithful daughter.
So I stored the fire inside my heart.
I am partially sure that mamma will never go with any adultery relation.But still the question remains, why pappa let us. That was a bleeding wound for the past decades.The bondage a girl expect from her father was enormous. That care, that strength and the warmth was the supreme power for a girl
And for me piyush is actually playing that role.Only he has the authority over me, only he cares me. And I behaved like a kid in front of him.But time passes he didn't call me back on that day. My heart finds some reasons favorable to him.
He may busy with family
He may didn't get privacy to call.
May he tried to call me back, and call wasn't connected.
I try to believe that.
But some crakes occur in my thoughts and that lead to my past, about the disappear of the favorite persons of my life.
I about to fell down deeply into the volcano of my past, soon, Mamma called me.
Miku, someone is calling you.
It was about 10 pm, we usually sleep at that time.

I ran to mamma's room and she handover her mobile to me by
        looking at me with fire in eyes.
I took the phone,not caring about mamma's fierce look.
I said politely,
Hello and slowly moved to the direction of my room.
Is there any problem to talk to you at this time?
He asked genuinely.
Yes.it is. but now I don't care.
Eh?
He laughed.
Where are you now?
At home.
Yeah that I know, exactly where, in your room.?
Yes.
My heart thrilled.
I was totally busy today.That is why I called you at this time. I
grumbled.
Now Say it again.
What?
That you said afternoon over phone, I didn't hear it clearly.
He mocked an innocent tone.
I smiled and blossomed.
Oh, nothing sir, I just asked you how is the weather there, is it
raining?
I was in a kiddish mood.
Oh, please stop this childish nature Nayamika,Say it clearly,
I want to hear completely.
I acted innocently.
What?
Don't know.?
 Then ok.bye
He shows a mocked frustration.
Don't go Piyush,please.
I melted and afraid that he may leave by cutting the call.
Then?You are not saying anything. How long I have to wait for
you?
I smiled. I feel I am blessed.
He changed his tone to a fake complaint.

What I need to say?
I am not insisting you, but you can say the truth that you love
me.
Who told you?
You..you..

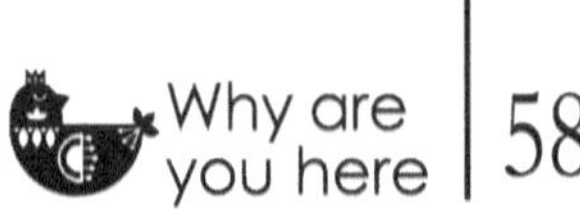

No,

Yes.Your eyes. You can't hide love spreads over me by your eyes.

Piyush, will you leave me?

I feel an obstacle sucked on my throat. I was in an urge of crying.

No,never.what happen? Why you are asking like this

I am afraid Piyush, everyone I loved, will leave me one day.

Nayan,it will happen as our life is not controlled by us. It is done by the omnipotent who decides everything. Do you believe in god?

Now I have belief in god, as you are with me to balance all my miseries.

Then we can do is to love each other And I will promise you that I never leave you, how can I leave you Nayan, I love you so much, that you can't imagine. I fell in love with you at the moment I saw you, at that time I have no idea about you, your name, your character, nothing. But my soul gives me an indication that this is your girl.

really?

Yes dear. I have seen you at the time of admission procedure, that day you wore a white kurti with a black long skirt. You didn't look at me but I was there near you.while you are checking your rank in notice board ,I reach close to you and find your name. From there I am murmuring your name, during my sleep, my wake up.. I love you Nayamika, from my ancient births, love you.

My heart wrenched; my sound faltered.I cant say anything.

Nayan? Will you be with me, forever?

Piyush,I too love you Biyush. But I am afraid

Piyush.Everyone leaves me, my pappa, chacha, I have no friends…Tears rolled from my eyes.

Piyush stood silent.

..I was alone Piyush..no one is there to love me, care me, totally alone.

Do you know Piyush, I liked to be talkative, actually I am, but nowadays I can't talk to anyone. I can't create a friend's zone..i create a shell and ..and you made me come out from it..

I cried and talked continuously.

I know Nayamika..i know everything. i love you Nayamika..

love you.. I am here for you till my death.

Tears dropped like an avalanche breakdown.

I am with you nayamika..i am with you..love you..ummahh.. I feel I am blessed than ever.

I closed my eyes to feel his love. I imagined he kissed my forehead and patted on my shoulders to placate me.I sense his love,that wasn't a teenage,time pass love or attraction.for me, it was divine, it was pretentious.

20

Mamma's Reaction about Love

On the very next day mamma looked at me with exasperation. She was very irritated by my behavior on the last night.I talked over mobile for a long time at night.But I was happy, never her anger can destroy my peace of mind.

I feel the emotion of every lover.They are on the sky not on the earth, none of the problems on the earth will trouble them, they only think about their soulmate and live in a different love world.I also enter to the world of love my holding Piyush's hands.I melted when I hear Piyush's sound.I never consider my mamma's anger while talking to Piyush.But Her behavior towards me become worser and worser.

one day when I return from entrance coaching class, I feel tired and fizzy.Just I reach the home, I feel some water is secreted in my throat and a sudden urge of omitting occurs.Mamma ran towards me.Within a second, she pushed my shoulders with anger.I fall towards the chair and it pains me.

Sh..you bloody bitch.. you spoiled your life,when did everything happened between you and him.

I sat on the chair and looked at her with affliction. I feel she was in an abnormal state. She left there by hitting her head, by her hands.I looked at her pathetically.

How can I tell her that loving someone won't let me to make pregnant?

I didn't say anything as I am tired. But I want to explain her about my love. On the next day, I didn't go to the institute and mamma was also at home.
I sat opposite to her.
Actually I feel angry about her last day's statement.
But I control myself.
Mamma, it was Piyush whom I called at that night.
I can see a fire in her eyes.
She didn't say anything. she just looked at me fiercely.
Mamma ,he cares me like a father and don't forget that everygirl wants their parent's care, I missed it and now …
Oh..do you know one thing, every wife needs a husband, and where is mine? Your dad, and still, you are waiting and crying for our dad's love, then who am I?You don't know struggles I have faced.
Mamma, I know..but
it was Piyush who give this strength of not getting angry.
Mamma and one more thing, it's just love, and why are misunderstanding me.
Hmm,,love, do you know your pappa and me loves each other and get married.and….
Mamma,will you please stop this, Piyush is not like any other man.
She mocked me with a smile.
And I promise you that what you afraid, that things never happened between us.
Oh, so you know everything in this seventeen th age, how do you know about those things.? You bloody bit..ch
Oh..is this my mamma? What happened to her.
I keep my patience only because of Piyush.Now I realize she cannot understand the depth of my love, my struggles.I know she hasn't walk through a smooth path of life.But for me, my priorities are important.
Mamma continued her words..
I have no one, my husband abandoned me, my daughter for whom I struggled everything is going to leave me, no relatives, no one..no…
Mamma, why you are thinking like this.i said everything to you, I can hide it, but never tried, I want my mamma should know about this.
About what?
Piyush loves me and I too love him.

Oh, so you both planned everything, then what is your parent's role.
We didn't planned anything, mamma.but if I marry,then it will be with Piyush.
If I marry ,then it will be with Piyush.. she mocked me by imitating my words
If I marry..if I maary….
Those words echoed in the surroundings.
Once you will realize, all men are selfish and they are just flirting with women for their own needs.
But not Piyush.
I replied and move back to my room.
She was in an anger and showed some abnormal behavior. May due to her past rejections and miseries. I feel happy that I can control my anger, frustration, sadness if Piyush is with me.

21
She Wakes up from her Past Dream

When I opened my eyes, I feel I was in a time machine and went back to my past, actually I slept here yesterday, Near holy Yamuna, under an unknown tree on a bare large stone.
It was really nice to be alone, and enjoying self-love.
She smiled herself.
when I am out of my depression, I am the happiest women and I want to freeze that mind setting like that till my death.
But without my permission, without any reason the depression wind blows mostly in every month, that time I lose my control, my dignity, my internal peace; it is totally like a volcano eruption.It only stops when I close my eyes and recollect any past memories with Piyush.Still, that is the therapy I am doing for myself.
I don't know where is he now, how he looks like, what he is doing.
But I will control myself not to think about Piyush, then also when my depression arrives and it only under controlled when I finally capitulate Infront of my soul and allow it to think about Piyush.
I recollect the memories happened before fourteen years, it wasn't difficult, because I have nothing to remember after we separate.
I didn't score much in entrances.
I didn't get seat for engineering or medicine in aided colleges.

We moved back to our house as chacha left there.
I didn't want to live there, as I have memories with pappa there.I
didn't want to stay in our rented house as I have memories
with Piyush there.I want to leave the place.
So I agreed to join for Bsc nursing, I don't know about my passion,
so I obeyed mamma.I behaved like a robot who moves
with the orders of others and having no self-esteem. I
studied hard, do the duties perfectly, and enjoyed the life
when I am around the patients.
Often, I went to home,
There I mostly welcomed with some maami's or distant relatives
as mamma is staying at our family house.
Usually they complain me that I didn't call or visit mamma, as
she dedicated her life for me.
I smiled and move forward if I am mentally stable.
But if I am not,I may lose my temper, I might lose my patience,
i may feel insomnia as it may give sparks to my past
residues.I can come out of mood swings only when I think
about Piyush and I image that I am saying my present
problem to him and he is consoling me in a different
manner.But I feel sheepish. Why I am thinking about a
person who abandoned me in a misery.
I want to come out from my melancholy by myself.
I tried to replace Piyush by some other persons, but it won't fit
properly.
Soon after I realized that no one can replace the position Piyush.
He influences me even if we separated or not talked for years.
She smiled,Did a women can love a man like this?
What will happen, if he loves me back like this.

I will roam around him,as like moon revolves around earth. I
will forget myself when I am with him and my smile will
be a reflection of his love, like moons light.
Did he miss me, ever? No, if yes, he will at least try to contact
me.
Then why me, God. I too need to get out of this.
I too need to forget him, I will go for a devotional mind therapy
for that. I am sure, this Kedarnath can erase all the past
forbidden thoughts from my mind. I took a deep breath, I
got the smell of devotional spirit. I want to forget about
me, please allow me to get out of his attractive power.

22

An Unexpected Meeting

How peaceful the atmosphere is, no one is complaining to God, no one is living with died soul, no one is thinking about the money,or any other valuable things they have or had.I can see a common thing in all their faces, tranquility.The soothing vibration is spreads around each and every person in Kedarnath.They are not thinking about their physical wealth they made in this life struggle, they are not having any arrogance about whom they are, they are not praising or cursing their kids, not even worrying about their own problems. They are in a persistent calmness.

I too want that harmonious feel.

I don't want to be tensed, whatever happened.

I don't want to cry or break my heart.

I hate to become ananxious woman.

I want to live peacefully without caring anything.

Whatever happen around me I don't want to break my peace.

I am obsessed with this atmosphere, they air, this peacefulness of my mind.

I deeply breath the air.

Someone patted slightly on my shoulder, I turned back.

That was a monk, dressed in saffron dothi with long mustache and beard, mostly white in color, but his eyes look like he was very young, vibrant.

He smiled at me.

Are you in search of someone?
No.
Are you looking for an answer?
No.
Then?
I am troubling to erase some past memories.
Why I say like that, I don't know.
Come with me.
I obediently followed him
He led me to a secluded place where I can see a temple like
building partially filled with snow.
Where we are going?
To get all answers of your queries.
It was dark inside the naturally built cave, I have seen a sage
who is under meditation, and the person who brings me
inside is now not there at all.
I turned around, some other people are also doing medication
and I can't see them properly due to less light in that
area.Then from darkness inside the cave, a person is
walking by holding a lamp in his hand, when he come
closer to me, he smiled and look deeply into my eyes in
search of something which he has missed somewhere.
I feel faint, my head started to spin.
Yes.when my eyes saw him, suddenly my mind whispered
Piyush.
It was Piyush.
His face become thinner; his beard grows up. But there is no
change in the intensity of his eyes that drowned me
completely.I feel I will fell down, so I sat on a rock piece
and Piyush sat on the floor.
I didn't spoke to him for a while. He looked intensively to my
eyes. Why, why are you here?
I asked in a low voice.
To see you.
The reply was crisp like always.
For what?
I have no answer for that question,nayamika.
He moved closer to me and place my face on his hands he moved
his face closer to me and kissed me on my forehead.
I still love you Nayamika,
In that moment, when he touches me I have no idea about what
to say, what to do. I didn't resist his movement. I closed
my eyes and fell down to the past dream.

But within a second, a flash of past memories rushed into my
        brain.
I moved back.
Piyush, I am leaving..
I stood up from the rock
I am here to meet a baba, who can say the life destiny.
I can tell you the destiny,Nayan.
I looked at him, he pranked me with his same cute expressions.
But I am not interested Piyush.
It was an involentary response.
His face changed,
I know you are angry with me
No piyush, I have no anger, no love, nothing towards you. His
face become gloomy he shook his head.
Nayan, I never abandoned you.
I closed my eyes in order to control my wrath.
He put his hands over my leg as he is asking for a pardon. My
heart wrenched.
Nayan,do you know what happened, during these years? I was

        actually behind you.but I have no courage to face you.
        The father is a follower and close friend of rishi kanth
        and I get to know about you from him. As he already
        knows about you, when he feels a connection while
        hearing your name, he called me and inform me about
        you.
Now do you belief in me?
What he was saying may be true but I don't want to go back
        and become the same Nayamika as he had.
Ok.I believed you. now allow me to leave
Nayamika, what happened.why ..why you are leaving.
Nothing Piyush. I am not the same Nayamika, as time passes, I
have changed a lot.
Actually I was not changed a bit but I am in a transition state.
But..but..i am still the same Piyush, who loves you a lot.
But. I can't.
Don't lie Nayamika. I can see your love towards me in your eyes.
No.no piyush. I have to go.
Ok,please listen, let me explain what happens during this years.
No need Piyush. I have no complaints.
But, I am ..I need you..please
His sound become soft, and genuine I feel if I wait there, I will
return to the past Nayamika, who madly in love with
Piyush.no, I don't want to become that girl.
I am going Piyush.

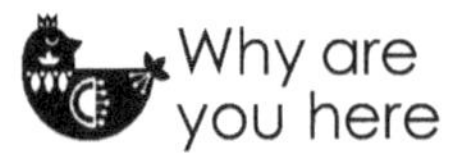

He takes his hands from my legs; I feel I lost the last warmth in my body but I have to go.

I ran from there as fast as I can. I didn't turn back to see him. He has such a power and that attracting me towards him strongly.

My mind changed a bit while feeling his love.But my brain won't allow me to go back to the previous life.

23
The Necessary Relieve

She sat near to Chorabari lake. Blue Himalayan anemone flowers blossomed there makes the area an enchanting beauty. But I wonder there was no bees attracted to it and none roaming around it. Their sunning appearance may attract everything towards it but why there is no bees.
I review a flower. I bring it close to my nose, oh , it doesn't have a smell and found they haven't produce any nectar.
Not all the flowers are following a common behavior, some of them have their own strange etiquettes.
To avoid the souvenir of Piyush, I tried to think about anemone flowers who are smiling at me with great passion.
Then I heard a mellifluous voice.
Why are you here beta?
I turnedback.
It was a woman in her middle age, whom I feel familiar. She wore a white saree and didn't put any make up, I feel like she was an angel.
I am just..i nodded my head for her to understand I have nothing to say.
She sat near to me.
I know you are worried?
No, I am not.
I can read you Nayamika,
She Patted by back.The touches are very important for me hence I feel an affinity towards her.
Who are you ,matha ji.

I am what you called me, mataji
Why beta, why are you here.
I don't know., I am not following a satisfied life. I don't know.
something is dragging me back .
She holds me tightly and moved her fingers over my head.
My eyes become wet.
Literary I need a harm hug like this. But I never get when I
need that. Usually Indians, think that touching is only for sex.
We prefer minimum body contacts. A mother never hugs
her adult male son as she afraid that he may feel any
sextual affinity!
A father too never touches her daughter after her body grown
up as the effect of hormone changes!
What a pathetic level of thinking.
Tough is very important for every human. Not only for humans,
all the living organisms need a safe touch in order to feel
the love.
I too feel an affinity towards that lady, whom I called mata ji.
So I said everything that hurts me.
I failed in everything. I failed in getting care from parents, family,
I lost the belief in love, I lost the devotion towards
god.now..i am totally alone.
She smiled.Her eyes show her clear thoughts
You came to earth alone, and God is appointing everyone in
this world for an obligation. But only a few, a very few
find the obligation and making their life satisfied. Rest of
all are frustrated,irritated and following something else
that actually wasn't their proper duty.
Yeah ,I too don't know about my obligation of life.
She moved her fingers over my hair.
You will find it soon. god will…
I didn't allow her to complete the sentence.
God wont. If god is there, then why I am supposed to face all
the struggling. I was hurting all the time by everyone I love I
have showed my irritation towards the life.
She didn't answer for that.
Everyone must face some miseries and pleasure, and the
ratio will be same for everyone.
No way mataji. I don't think so, I have faced a lot than no one
else in the world
No.beta, then You tell me the tragic situations in your life.
I looked at the great Himalayas, and answer.

My struggle begun when pappa left us..tears are incontrollable and it flows from eyes and then from nostrils too.
She closed her eyes.
If pappa won't leave you, he will make so many nuisances to you. He was an extravagant and he will sell everything you have. And do you know one more thing, if he was there, your mom won't try for a job and his family will not allow her to go for job. And also, there is a high chance that he will become alcoholic and may finally you will totally hate him, if he won't leave.
She tries to go back to her past.
She feels it may be correct, if pappa won't leave us,I may not get the care as I have expected .
She feels a relaxation.
Next,
Mata ji looked at my eyes.
If chacha wont make the problem, I will be so attached to chacha and I may not free like this.he will start controlling you over what you wear, what you study whom you talk like that..
I find the solution for my second stone which I held in my heart.
I feel a relaxation but I have to ask about Piyush. Why he abandoned me?
Piyush?
She didn't allow me to complete it,
Close your eyes and think Nayamika, will you happy if Piyush be with you?

24

Memories of the
Last Meeting

I recollected the time I spend with Piyush. After the conflict with mamma about Piyush, I called him and asked him that I need to meet him. He came near to the institute, I ran towards him with extreme happiness.

Eh? Are you not afraid madam?

About what?

If somebody get to know about our meeting?

I don't care.

Eh?ha ha ha

He laughed by looking at my eyes.

You want to say something?

Yes. will you marry me?

Now?

he mocked me by smiling and look deeply into my eyes.

No, I am asking seriously.

Oh..madam.

Please give the answer?

How can I promise you dear? This is life, so everything is unpredictable.

What do you mean?

It means, I will try to make everything happen, I want to get the permission from my family., they must allow me to marry a girl

Means?

I scrutinized him. I feel a pain.

If they won't allow, then?

He smiled, then..he showed that he was thinking by bending
 his neck and looked up .
What do you mean by that.
That word belch from inside, and I feel a shivering in my body.
Hey..Nayamika..cool..
He didn't sense the seriousness in my words.
If you give a kiss on my lips, I will think about marrying you?I
lose my temper.
so one day you leave me unnoticed. that words not came
from me, it was involentary.
He showed a mocking face.
Ey, Nayan I am just kidding. don't take it as a matter of
 importance.
Piyush, I am serious. I told my mom that you love me and I too
 love you.
So what? Its good that not to hide your love from others.
So I need the answer, if some problem occurs in marriage what
 will you do
I will hold you tightly and will declare this is my girl and I will
 die if you didn't agree with the marriage
 He showed some dramatic action and I feel he is still mocking
 me.
Will you please stop this?
Ey, cool my girl. I love you, that you know and there will be no
 change in the amount of affection I have shown to you.but
 marriage is not a silly thing. We have to grow up and we
 have to consider our family too.
Ok. So?
So be cool my girl.
If they wont let you ,then?
Don't think too much Nayamika.
So,you will also leave me, right?
As I feel he was sneering at me.
But,I lost my mind, I fainted, I imagined the day , when he leaves
 me. So better to leave him at this moment. No need to
 encourage my affection.As soon as a bus arrived at the
 bus stop I ran and get into it, without saying anything to
 Piyush.
Piyush didn't understand what happened around him at the
 moment.
Why she left?I didn't say that I won't marry her.My love towards
 her is genuine and sincere. Why this silly girl dubious
 about my love?

She said she came after quarrelling with mom.so may she was in an emotional trauma; I didn't ask her about that. I didn't care her in a better way. I have to give more strength to my girl then only she will sustain. That much she loving me.He took a deep breath and looked at her, she was inside the bus and didn't look back.

He smiled. What an Imbecilic girl! I have to say her that don't love me this much, that makes me mad.

As she reached home, at the same moment, she blocked his number in the phone and deleted every digital memory about him.

Before deleting she read all the messages he send to her,and by hearted it.

I don't want to get cheated. but It will be hard for me to forget him.

My first love, first person cares me, values me...

The first day I lied to my mom that I am suffering from headache and spend most of the time in the bed.On the second day I can't sleep and my eyes started to shed tears, I tried to hide it a lot.But whenever I am seeing the phone, I feel Piyush may trying to call me several times, soon I unblocked his number.I have waited the whole day by expecting his call.I again feel auditory hallucination, as I am hearing his sound, I ran to verandah and he was not there.He can call me, how he can stay happily without talking to me?

So his love was not genuine.

I again blocked his number with an utter cry. I closed my mouth forcefully with my palm.The days begins and ends slowly, most of the time I spend by thinking about Piyush.

After about two weeks, the day before my entrance exam I can't concentrate on my studies, I take a decision to call Piyush.That was little hard for me, but I make me understand that for your favorite persons you can hide your attitude.I close the book and take the mobile and dialed his number.

It rings…rings…rings…

Finally, I heard a harsh hello from a person, who won't be Piyush.

Who are you?

I..i..

I cut the call, without saying anything.

I feel ashamed.
Why I called him?
It may be his father. Will he call me back? And if mamma attends, what will happen?As I feel afraid, I blocked his number.
I try to remove him from my mind. I give back mobile to mom.

> But the memories created by him was never ending. When I see rain, I will think about the first meeting with Piyush at my home. When I close my eye I can hear the sound of piyush. I took a piece of paper given by Piyush where he has written his number was now totally fainted because of my tears.Imiss him badly. I found this misery was more than I expected.Then I conclude, he didn't love you, like you did.

So, you don't try to contact him.

25
Tempting Soul

I tried not to remember about him but I can't.Every second if I am conscious I will think about him.I didn't get better scores in entrance exam so I joined for nursing.I even didn't try for any other career options as I am totally in a fed up state.

For me nursing was the low-grade job Even though mamma forced me to join for nursing. I can't resist her, because that time I was totally lost and depressed.I never enjoyed anything in hostel or class.But I studied everything.ThereI create a different Nayamika, who was bold, depressed, and loves solitude.I have studied govt nursing school, Trissur.

I know it was Piyush's area and i expect I will meet him one day.

I waited for four years, when I am in hospital duty, I expected he will come there and surprisingly we met and the love will restart. Never happened.

But in the last day in college, after completing exam, I took a deep breath and decided to go to his home as I feel I am totally tired of expecting him every day. Even if I saw him I can ask directly that he loved me or not.

Then I can get rid of this uncontrollable thoughts related to him and I may feel a peacefulness.

What his mother will say, when i reach there ?

Nothing wrong in going and meeting your friend.

When they open the door, I will introduce myself that I am Nayamika, and piyush was my school mate.

And if they doubtfully look at me, then I will say, I need a help from piyush's side that I need to find a ladies hostel during my intership. So I came here to meet him.

Better. I planned everything briefly.
I don't know the exact place of his house, but I know his house
         name.I hire an auto and went to his area.
Driver dropped me exactly Infront of the house, but
         Before leaving he asked,
Why you are here madam?
I looked at him by aiming why he asked that question to me.
Madam, if you came here to meet doctor Prabhakar, he is not
         here, no one is here, they have shifted their house and
         moved to Delhi.
I looked at the large bungalow with giant gate. Paint was fainted
         and the yard was messy. Yes, what he said maybe true.
Why?
I don't know, my house is nearby and for the last two years I
         didn't saw anyone here. I think they went with his elder
         son who went to Delhi for pursuing MBBS. And someone
         said they are going to sell this house.
I totally lose my patience.
Letsgo,brother. I get into the auto, as I saw a car is coming to
         the area.
To avoid unnecessary questions from rickshaw driver, I took
the headphone from my handbag and fitted to my ears.

Parayathe ariyathe nipoyathalle, maruvakku mindaanjathalle..
Orunokkukaanathe nipoyathalle, dooreykku nimanjathalle..

A Malayalam song apt to the situation, she think, he also leaves

         me without saying a word, without meeting each other
         for a last time as like in this song.

Why Piyush cheated me by showing a mountain of love towards
         me.? He can at least call and tell me that he is moving to
         Delhi.My landline number is still active.Yes, he is a
         cheater. tears rolled inside and get ready to burst.

Words From Piyush

Piyush feel tired,after the long journey.He was actually
smelling the kerala weather. As he always miss kerala when he
was
at Delhi. The rain, the warmth, the greenery and my girl. Not
only kerala, I missed all my favorite things during the past 4
years.
Mostly my girl, Nayamika. He feels a quite unexpected hurry in

meeting her.I have to say sorry to her. How much my girl
will get worried as I am unexpectedly abandoned her. I
know it may pathetically destroyed her soul. How should
I have to say a sorry? by giving a tight kiss on her lips.
I smiled suddenly the smile fades away, in this four years of
oblivion, did she finally decide to move forward with
someone else?
No.no.its my Nayamika. if years or decades of oblivion never
separate her from me.
As I saw a ricksaw infront of our house, I simply think, may it
be Nayan.
Soon the ricksaw turned around and I noticed a girl inside that,
who was finding something from her bag.
I can't believe in my eyes,I patted on my hand.
Pappa..please stop the car. I quickly open the door and come
out of the car by uttering, please stop the rickshaw.
But my sound isn't reach there, they moved fast.
Pappa, mamma it was Nayamika. I saw her.
Pappa and mamma looked at each other.
Ok.cool Piyush. She is here, we will find her for you.
I couldn't control my excitation. Shebecame thin, I feel, I have
only seen her side face, she may be still searching me, that's
why she is here.
Pappa and mamma passed a pale smile.
Piyush, we will find the girl at any cost. At least I have to do
that for my son.
After pappa's declaration, mamma looked at him with a sad
smile.
How much he has suffered, she murmured. Piyush get back to
car and recollect his past memories. He never tried to dig
it as it hurts him

26
His Memories
of the Last Meeting

The day when she left bus stop without saying anything, I
received a call from mamma.
Piyush, beta, Prithvi fell down while playing football and he
has some head injuries, get a bus and come fast
Oh,don't be panic mamma, nothing will happen to Prithvi, it
may be a silly injury, and where he has admitted?
He is at karuna hospital and pappa is going their from his
hospital
Ok. Mamma. I will come soon.
I rushed and catch a bus to Trissur without informing any of
my friends.
I get inside the bus, my was heart wrenching , don't trouble us
god, please make his alright soon. I think about to call
Nayamika, I took my mobile and her's was switched off.
I keep my mobile on my hand
Within fifteen minutes my phone vibrates, and I looked at it, it
was a call from pappa, not Nayan.
Pappa, I am coming.
Hello. Who is this?
Who are you? This is my dad's number.
Yeah. I am Trissur town SI, arun. piyush, your dad met
an accident and he is unconscious now.
What? I can't believe my ears.
What? I repeated the question.
Yes Piyush. Will you inform your mom or..I?
No, no sir. I will come soon.

An eighteen year old boy within the gap of fifteen minutes
become pathetically down, and always he believed that
he was the luckiest person who got a wonderful family.
He rolled his fingers and moved it closer to mouth to control
his tears.
He finally gains some energy to call mamma.
Piyush where are you ? have you got the bus?
Yes mamma.Mamma, pappa called me and he said he can't
come to karuna hospital now, as he has an emergency
work at the hospital.
I said the lie in a single statement.
Oh, he didn't call me,
Ha, he said, he tried to call you, but it wasn't connected.
Ok. I will hire an auto and will go to Prithvi.You come fast Piyush,
I am afraid Piyush , I am shivering.
Ok.mamma, be calm. Nothing will happen. Don't worry.

I feel every second is moving like hours. I cant imagine Prithvi's
face or pappa's face. When I reached at the hospital where
pappa is working, there he was admitted now.
I rushed to the room. He was sitting on the bed, and there was a
cloth tied over his head.
Pappa..pappa..
My voice gets blurred.
Nothing Piyush, nothing happened to me,
I rushed to him and hug him.
He patted on my shoulders.
Nothing piyush. You have to be more strong.
His sound was stumbling, I noticed it
What happened pappa, anything series about prithvi.
I scrutinized him.
Nothing.prithvi is fine. I have contacted the doctor.
Then?
Piyush, have to be stay calm.
Yes pappa, say what happened?
My car hit a boy on the road, and his condition is critical.
Oh, don't worry pappa. You didn't do it intentionally.
I feel a relaxation that my pappa and Prithvi are fine.blood is
thicker than water, I didn't think about the person who
was injured critically in the accident.
Still I saw an annoyance on pappa's face.
Pappa.dont worry. I will go to the person and will give any kind
of support, money or anything.

Piyush, are you forgot about my post-doctoral fellowship at
      Beckenhamon this Friday.
Oh, I actually forgot about incident.
That was pappa's dream.
What is the problem in going for that? I will take care of
Prithvi and mamma.
I behavied like an mature enough to manage the situation.
Dear, this is a criminal case and I am the suspect and I am not
      supposed to go abroad.
Oh, I didn't think about that, so what we will do pappa?
I don't know son,
He moved his fingers over piyush's hair.
Pappa. Can I attend for the bail? Can we say that I drove the
      car and I will be the suspect and you can go, right?No,
beta, no. it's not fair.
Why pappa. We are not cheating. I will inform the police.
Pappa stood silent. I feel at least I have to do this for my dad,
he lived for us.
We have resolved the issue, and police informed that pappa can

      go to Buckenham on Friday.We both reached at Prithvi's
      place and we didn't inform anything related to this issue,
      to Prithvi and mamma.Pappa was still worried and
      continuously contacting the hospital for getting the recent
      updates about the victim.

By the next evening pappa went to Buckenham and mamma
      and me stayed with Prithvi.I didn't contact Nayamika
      for the last twenty-four hours, my mobile was switched
      off and I didn't have my charger. I took mamma's
      mobile and come out of the hospital room, by typing a
      message to her, straight away I saw a bunch of police
      men are approaching me.

Piyush.please be quiet and listen to me.
One of the cop said gently.
I keep mobile locked and looked at them.
Yes, sir.
Piyush, your car hit a person and he died half an hour before.
Oh, god.
I rubbed my hands on the forehead.
Sir, so ?
So, Piyush now you are the culprit and we have to arrest you.
Sir, why? it was an accident sir.
Yeah.but it is found that the driver was violated traffic rule, so
      it is homicide.

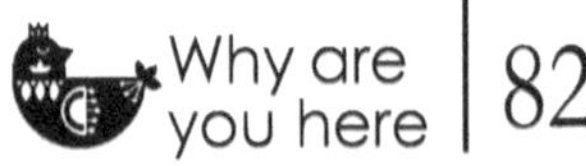

Oh, when pappa heard about the accident of Prithvi he may
        lost his mind, so may he violate rules.I was about to cry.
Don't worry piyush. you come with us.
Can I call my pappa?
Yes. You can.
I tried to call pappa again and again and then only I
        remembered, he was on the board.
One minute sir, I have to say to my mom.
I re entered the hospital room and moved towards Prithvi , and
        I hugged him and kissed his neck.
Mamma, please listen.yesterday pappa met an accident and the
        victim died just now. So, I have to go to police station.
    Oh.what Piyush, what are you saying. why you all hide that from
        me. He said it was a minor accident happened when car fell
on a pothole.
I didn't say anything.
I patted on mamma's shoulder and she was crying painfully. Stay
strong mamma, pappa will come within one week. Don't
        worry.
When I come out from the room, my eyes are filled with
        tears.That still flows like a never draining spring.

28
Life After Releasing from Prison

When I come out of the jail after six months of prison, I feel I totally lost my life. It was really a hell and all my courage to live this beautiful world has lessen. I never face any trouble till my 18 th birthday. My pappa and mamma never allow us to face a trouble, they were act us a shield for us. I never complain about the incident, I never incriminate pappa. It will be my faith. I have to face it anyway.Some problems are like that, you cant get rid of that. You have to face it boldly.

I tried to make my family happy. So as their request we shift to Delhi and I have joined for MBBS.

I totally miss Nayan, but I didn't call her. I feel I will meet her one day and will explain everything. After not using mobile for a long time, I found there is no need of mobile in life, so I just keep it, rarely attend calls, never call anyone.

During my first year MBBS degree, I was paralyzed with heavy fever during our class time. I was diagnosed with dengue fever at its high level.icant open my eyes as I want to do so. I totally bedridden for two days.

When I opened my eyes and got little strength, Prithvi looked at me with a strange smile. As mamma and pappa try to placate me, I looked at Prithvi and I didn't understand the reason behind his smile.

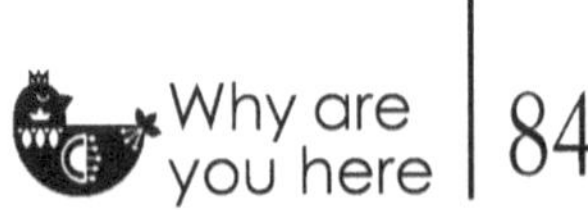

As they went out from the room, he starts croon a song, I feel that made by himself.

o..oo..naya..nayamikaa..

I miss you so much…..

I tried to smile, what are you saying,Prithvi, are you mad?

I am not mad, but found some others madness.

He always try to make me as like I am before going to jail I too act that I have no miseries in order to make my family happy.

What happened to you Prithvi?

Your secret lover..

He replayed with the same rhythm and start moving like a salsa dancer.

I feel little anxious, he said her name, how?

Yet I didn't say her name to Prithvi.

He again laugh and continues his song to mock me.

o…nayaaamikaa…

will you please stop this, paagal ?

I am not paagal, but you.

You secretly loves a girl..

Oh,,nayaamika…

He again moves by singing the song.

Oh, Prithvi..i smiled and try to hit him, as glucose drip is inserted on my hands, will cause a pain.

Aaa..

As he noticed, I was paining, he stops the dance and move closer to me and with a husking sound he said.

You said it bro.yesturday night,

What?

I miss you nayamika, I need you. And ummaahhh..

He mocked like he is trying to kiss me.

I closed my eyes, to hide my shyness.

Is it true or he is lying?

I scrutinized him, but he shows an innocent face.

But I never said her name to him, or to anybody at home.

I miss her, that is true. More than anyone, my mind knows that.

Will pappa and mamma hear that?

Yes,of course. Two nurses are also heard that.

I mocked some actions to humiliate me.

I expect mamma or pappa will enquire me about nayamika, but they never asked me about that. But I have explained everything to Prithvi and he always forces me to call her.

Finally one day, Prithvi passed a message for me to mamma.

Mamma, piyush wants to meet that girl.
Mamma stood silent and look at me. I feel she was expecting
the question from the last 3 years.
After a moment, she said.
Piyush I am afraid about you. Will a girl wait for her lover for
three or four years without any communication?
I have no answers for that.
Mamma continued, if that girl is engaged with someone else,
then also you have the courage to face it. I don't want to
see you in a lost mind again beta, I don't want you to face
any more struggles, you already had a lot.
Mamma cried silently and mamma and pappa get to know
everything from Prithvi about nayamika and they decided
to go to kerala and meet her.
Before going pappa said one thing,
If we didn't met her, or she engaged with anyone else, you have
to forget her. don't spoil your life for love.
I promised to him that if she engaged with someone else, I never
say a word related to nayamika after that. I cant promise
him that I never think about her.
I feel I have seen her,she was travelling in a rickshaw, but I am
not sure, as I was seeing her in my dreams every time.
For us it was difficult to find her as she left her old rented house
and move back to their ancestral home. She was not in
contact with any of our friends so finally as a last attempt,
I visited the hospital where she completed her bachelor
of nursing that said one of our plus two teacher. From
there I got an information that she was going to
Uttarakhand.

She can contact me, I have never changed my contact number.
So, I failed in finding her and we returned to Delhi. Prithvi
patted on my back and say that once I will met her. I hold his
hands tightly.
Prithvi,I have lost my confidence about life

No, piyush. You will get her Uttarakhand isn't too far from delhi.
He always call me as piyush from childhood and when pappa
and mamma tried to correct it, I rejected,he must be my
friend so better to call me by my name.
As I expected, he is my strength and he continued his search for
Nayamika

29

The Desire to
Finish Life

Day by day I become weaker and weaker. If I think about Piyush, I cant come out from the love whirlpool. I tried a lot. But I melts, when I think about him.My mind creates strong reason for the disappear of Piyush in order to love him. My life become more sorrowful after the disappearance of Piyush.

After completing the intership I have attended so many interviews in multispecialty hospitals. Even I have more potential than my classmates, my application got rejected by the interview board. I feel I have attended well, but I didn't receive offer letter.

I failed in first interview, I cried throughout the night and at the moment mamma called me in order to know the result of the interview.

I was broken and said painfully

 mamma, I didn't get it

I was sure that she wont console me,

She replayed,

I am an unlucky lady and now I feel my daughter too. I am dying to pay the amounts of the loan from bank that we hire for your studies. You are not failed miku, but I am.

That killed me.

Soon my mind recollected all the incidents faced on my life.

My father leave me, my relatives didn't like me, I have no friends, I was cheated by Piyush..i was rejected in the job interview…

I cried.. I cried.. my pillow was flooded with my tears.

Soon, I remembered, the same pillow I hugged by considering that was Piyush.Soon I have a strong desire to talk to Piyush.
I wiped my tears.
I take the mobile and dialed his number after a couple of years.
My heart pumps blood faster than its usual rate.The call got connected.
When I tried to call him after that , it wont connect .So I thought Piyush won't use that number.
My body was shivering when I heard his sound.
Hello…
It was Piyush.I closed my eyes and tears rolled from it.I cant say anything.
In the second time, when he spoke, hello..
I replied, Piyush..i am…..
I couldn't complete it , soon he got nervous.
Na..nayamika.how are you? .i .. I am..sor..sorry..please..please pardon me..
I cut the call,I didn't open my eyes.Tears dropped
continuously from it.
I switched off the mobile.
No need to talk to him again.
What a fool am I?
Why I am here?From my birth, I am suffering. I don't…I
don't want to live here.. he didn't atleast enquired about me for these years, then also I called him, what a shameless person am I?
I took a large sigh.
Yes. The thought accidentally came to my mind. But, my tears stopped when I get the spark. Yes, I have to leave this world. That is my revenge, god.
I didn't write any death notes. Everyone will get confused to find the reason behind my death.
I saw the sharp knife in front of my table, that we brought for cutting fruits.
None of my roommates are there.
Perfect time for dying.
May police will call Piyush, but that won't make him into trouble, as we didnt spoke anything.
He may say Nayamika was my friend, and why she called me that I don't know, soon the call disconnected.
I take the knife, as a nurse, I know how to make the perfect wound to kill myself.

I bring the knife near to my wrist.
As I expected, there was a knock in the door. God never allow
me to escape from this suffering.
I opened the door.
It was our matron.
As soon as I opened the door,she peeped into my eyes.
Are you crying?
No,something fell into my eyes.
The most familiar lie.
Your madam called and informed that there will be an interview
tomorrow to Oman king Fahad hospital in kochi at 9
am. She tried to call you but your mobile was switched off.
She said everything in a second and returned.
I get into my room.
I smelled a positive spirit.
May I didn't get today's interview because God decided me to
get a job at Oman.
Mamma will say I am lucky if I got it.
I changed the plan of suicide.
I feel better.
I switched on my mobile.
I have seen ten call notifications and thirteen text messages by
Piyush.
I blocked his number.
I don't want you, cheater.

30

Off to dev Bhumi

I was happy and I have strong feeling that I will proud of myself
if I get that job and will follow a satisfied life.
I attended the interview I have answered almost everything they
asked, they was happy and they give me a shake hand
and said will contact you ,if selected.
I feel proud.
I hopefully believe that they selected me.
I will earn money and will follow a happy life in Oman.
I expected their call on the next day, next week,next month.
I finally realized that I rejected in that interview too.
I didn't yelled.
But cried silently in the bathroom.
Next job interview, next, next…
I failed, I rejected, I could attend due to fever.
Opportunities came and make me to dream about that and
finally flies off.
Later, it become my habit.
Attending interviews, failing, returning, repeat.Everyone
including my friends confused about the reason behind
the rejection of my application.
When I reach the bottom of sadness, I feel if Piyush is there, he
can help me to come out of this.I believe, only piyush's
words can make me out of all the sadness.But my self-
respect, won't allow me to call him.He also didn't call me
again, often I unblocked his number. And waited for his
call.

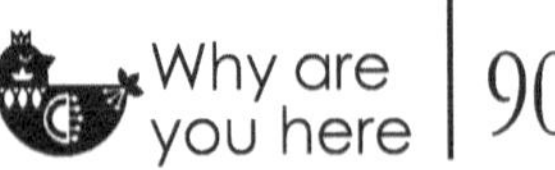

That time I got a job without interview in an old age home in Uttarakhand,Idecided to go for the job in order to move away from the people I know.

Everyone including my mom continuously torturing me by asking about my interview results.

I tried to ignore them.

But usually, I got hurt.

When I say mamma about the job I got in Uttarakhand, she yelled by saying that,

For the job you got, you no need to pass bsc nursing, just a homenursing certificate is enough.

Before hearing the unlucky girl quote, I left home.

My neighbors stopped my way.

You go and meet x or y, who is a rich and staying abroad, he or she can help you to get a job.

I ignored.

I didn't get any aid, when I need that.So I cant indulge anyone for helping me.I gain the courage to face all the questions.I feel I become rebel against the entire society.Some of my distant relatives came and advised me to do a post-graduation in nursing.I smiled because, I know, the loan amount of bsc is ascending day by day.I cant afford it.

Some of them giving me a ..for getting married.

If you marry a rich man, or a person with government job, all your miseries will come to end.

I thought, can money make me happy?

Some signed that may I have a boyfriend, for him, I going to Uttarakhand.

Some cried, she wasting her life by searching for jobs.

Some murmured, did she pass the B.Sc. nursing?

If yes, why didn't get job.my relative, some p or q got the visa to Canada or France.

She may have some interview fears

Going to Uttarakhand was not my dream, as I have no dream, but still I take the decision to go, to get rid of the people surrounding me.

31

The Warmth of Divine Home

Uttarakhand is known as dev Bhumi and I feel it was the perfect name we can give.It is the part of western Himalayas lying on its lap and everywhere is Himalayas.I wondered, how beautiful is our india.People nowadays usually believe that India is dirty having less facilities, Indian currency has less value,india is still economically developing country, we cant earn anything.so better to go for Europe or America.

But when I reached there, I feel it was the spectacular moment in my life.

Nature was at its full energy, every corner of Garwal, where the oldage home, divine home, is located, is full of blossomed trees and plants.

My eyes feel relaxed there.divine home is a small building as I expected, it was about 150 people.They are not bedridden, but my duty is to do a usual checkup in every morning.

Later I will be free.

The divine home is just like a home, they wake up, cook food , plant trees, go out for regular shopping and I can see a relaxed smile in every face. I never seen this much happiness in the face of an adult above 60 year old. Their eyes have a sparkling power.

Even my eyes look older than them.

I passed exams for my speaking and listening skills in English for going abroad.. But I forget how to communicate in hindi, that I have learned upto higher secondary. so initially it was difficult for me to communicate in hindi, but they co operated a lot. I found that among them only a few knows hindi and others are speaking in some native languages. I wonder how they are communicating with each other.

They are very happy, laugh loudly and speaks a lot with each other.

I want to know about them, once I asked dev baba, who owned this divine home.whom I feel the most happiest fellow in the world.

Dada, why you are here?

Here? In order to make me happy.

You aren't happy at your own home

I was happy but I didn't feel a satisfaction,

Eh?

Why?

We can live in different ways, we can act like we are happy or we can make ourself happy.

So,

So, we start living here, before that we are struggling to live. Do you know, when I started this home, me and my two friends only stays there, now we all are one fifty.but when we reached here, living together we feel we became younger, we participated in rescue operation during calamities, we offer food for the refugees, we give shelter to all other persons at our age. When we were at different places , we all panicked by only expecting their death every time.but here, we feel more we are healthy, we feel more happiness,more love, more duties. We are happy here. we often visit our place and they also shocked by seeing this drastic change that happens internally and externally on everyone here.

He concluded soon but I feel he wants to say more.

Beta,why you are here?

Dada, its my job.

No, I am sure you didn't select this job.

Yes, dada.

I admitted.

Your eyes are not happy.

I smiled.

My eyes got wet.

I feel an affinity towards him.
I take a deep sigh.
Yes, dada, I am not happy about the job.
Why?
Because..because..most of my friends are in foreign countries
        and earning ten times as mine.
Hahahahah…
He laughed..
did he mocked me?
He just moved his hands over my hair.
Beti, money cant make you happy.
You are very blessed, find your own happiness and move on..
I got stucked..
I feel confused.
What makes you happy?
I have to think..
he smiled.
find it soon, you are wasting the time of your happiness.
I think about the question, what makes you happy?
Is that Piyush?

32

Home Coming of Pappa

I was dumbstruck for some time and returned to my room.
passively I open the lock of my mobile, it was a right-
angledtriangle from the first corner.
There I saw three missed calls of mamma.
Why she called me in this time, usually I call mamma in the
morning.
I called back.
She attended the call with a strange voice.
Miku..come back soon.
Eh? What mamma.
I found her voice is not panic, so no need to worry.
Miku..your pappa is here, I will give…
Without completing the sentence, she handed over the phone
to pappa.
Miku..my girl..become too big..yar…. I want to see you my
sweetie.
my entire body and brain got freezed
I found that it was my pappa.
However, I didn't say anything.
I cut the call and fell into the bed.
I cried, screamed, sobbed pull the pillows into my mouth in order
to control the sound.
I tried to stop it, however I failed.
Why I cried? I don't know. I tried to realize my mind, it was a
moment of happiness and why you are crying.
My mobile ringed again and again, I didn't pick the call.
I slowly rolled into the sea of Piyush.
I feel want to talk to him.
I didn't think about the hates I have towards him.
I only remembering how he treated me when I am in an unusual
situation.

I feel if Piyush was here, he can understand the reason
behind my tears,that I still didn't understand.
I took the mobile inorder to call Piyush, the same moment call
        from mamma came and accidentally I attended it.
Miku,why you are like this. What your pappa will think? He
        came back in order to see you
I didn't say anything.
Oh,now are you feeling that you don't want us,? You got the job
        and feels that you are secure, right? and remember one
        more thing, he needs your presence now, as he is not well
        and as you know, we can't afford a nurse for this
        requirement.
I smiled pathetically, and loose my temper.
Mamma, excuses, I too need the presence of a dad,but that time,
        no one was there,ok, please remember that.
I got shivered while saying those words, my voice raised my
        heart pumps blood faster than the usual rate.
Oh,what a hatred daughter I have, why you are thinking so
        differently.
I took a deep breath to control my anger.
Mamma, I am thinking how you can think differently, without
        knowing the other persons's feelings.
She didn't leave it.
If you are my daughter, you have to come and our dad spoke to
        MLA and will arrange a job for you at government
        medical college.
I don't want any job. I will live here.
With the trifle, what you can do for your future.Remember, I
        have spoiled my life for you.
I was totally in an argument mood.
Whom told you to spoil your life, why you didn't kill me, when
        father left us.
Oh..this is the best sentence a mother can get from her daughter.
        Good miku.
She cut the call as I didn't say anything for a second.
I don't want to say that, but she always thinks about the world
        around her.I usually don't go for an argument but here it
        was totally out of my control.
Why mamma changed like this, he abandoned us and how could
        he come back after two decades of years.
Am I a person who hates love?
What happen to me?
Why am I like this?

Why I talk to mamma like that?
She lived for me. I know. However, she behaves in a different manner, or me?
I am person who controlled by something else, may be a negative power.
Whom has the authority over me.
I don't know.
I don't know..
I cant sleep. I called mamma again.
She was in a seriousness tone, but I was in an edge of cry.
Miku, you come and see the situation of pappa, and hear what he can tell,then you will realize.
I didn't reply as I don't want to hear any explanation from pappa.
Why you didn't understand my situation? I want to live at least some days with you and your dad.
But..but..mamma, try to understand my situation.
What ..what miku? I can't understand you. Once you said, there was no one to care you from our family, now we want to care you but you are refusing it. You are only thinking about you,that's why..
I understood that it will lead to another argument.
Ok.bye mamma. I will call you back.I have some duties here. I cut the call.
It was late at night..I opened the windows. Far away, i can see the Himalayas. My mind tempts me to get a devotional care.
I imagined god siva, at the top of mountain and I feel I am seeing that like in DEVON KE DEV..MAHADEV..devotional drama. I heard the title song in my ears..i slowly, intentionally fell into the devotional spirit as I found I have no other strong shoulders to lay down.

Karpuraguaram,karunavatharam
Sansar   saram,   bhujagendraharam.
Karpuraguaram,karunavatharam
Sansar saram, bhujagendraharam
aa..saadavasantham..hridhayaarvinde.
saadavasantham..hridhayaarvinde
bhavambhavami,sahitamnamani
bhavambhavami,sahitamnamani

Soon, I took thephone and search for buses to Kedarnath, without thinking a bit I booked a ticket for the next day and informed the office for one week leave approvement.

33
Kedarnath

I need the presence of Piyush, for all my traumas, my weaknesses my pleasure. But I can't request him to love me, as my attitude admires me.Sometimes I think, what a different person is me, I am not loving anyone now, I am only thinking about me, like mamma said.For me it is difficult to forgive someone, as I need to do so, but I am not able to do so.I didn't give pardon to Piyush, not to my dad, even not to mamma, as she is using harsh words on me. But I love them all.

Why I am like this.

I don't know. My head is full of questions, my frontal lobe synapsis is continuously sending signals, so I feel even I connect a millivoltmeter to head, it shows some high voltages. I feel I need some citalopram medicine to get rid of these questions as it can slow down the thoughts.I tried to close my eyes. Even the bus is moving slowly, my mind reaches the top of Himalayas.

As the bus start moving through steep curves, I am getting a smell of Himalayas, I opened my nostrils and breath it as possible as I can.Actually, I feel it opened some of my closed rooms of happiness inside my brain. I feel my eyes are getting more oxygenated hemoglobin now as my vision become too clear and I feel some point of relaxation.What is this enchanting smell, which enters to my brain within seconds and it starts its action soon. Is that any drug?is that any dopamine?

I turned around, most of the passengers of the bus are middle aged person and some are sleeping and others are watching the beauty of himalyas.

I again moved my head upwards and smell it deeply, I can feel
 the pleasure now.
I smiled.
I feel a warmth .
 Everywhere is himalyas, the holy land where godsiva lived.
I smiled to myself, when I become a devotee, I don't know. But
 if all the persons in world rejects me, hates me, abandoned
me, I don't feel upset as I have god, who is omnipotent. I
laughed now.
Thank you God. I am blessed now.
Neither Piyush, nor my dad, can make me happy like this.
Because this is permanent happiness. I never want to return
 from this holy northern india, there I want to spend my
 entire life.
If Piyush is also with me?
Again I understood my thoughts are leading me to Piyush. But I
 don't think that it will be the thing makes me the happiest
 person. I didn't get the answer of your question dev baba.
What makes me the happiest creature in the world?
My mind knows that but my brain isn't discover it.

I expect this holy land will give me all the answers, I have to
 meet rishi kanth, a saint who can predict future as well
 as he can read our mind. eventhough, I can't read my
 mind, if he can do it, it makes me more confident and I
 will get an authority over my mind, I could control my
 thoughts. I am a follower of rishi kanth for the past two
 years, and there is a community created by the followers
 of rishi kanth and I informed them about my arrival,
 otherwise getting a chance to meet him is difficult.
Everyday from his channel we will get some thoughts, and that
 will be hit the correct points on the mind, may be a mistake
 we are repeating every day, he will update the methods
 to get rid of it.
Its not too religious, it isn't make us addicted with religion, it's
 a way of making us fulfilled in life. He always says the
 god isn't there for troubling us, he is their to guide us and
 through our mind the god communicates, in order to
 understand that we must have a faith, a fare soul, a
 peaceful atmosphere.
If our thoughts are filled with angry, envy, miseries,
 hopelessness, then we wont understand the god's
 communication as they act as the noise in the channel. So

first try to erase them all, make the path clear, then you can her the god.

In divine home, I have seen everyone is listening and discussing about his thoughts, I also feel it is valuable, hence I too become a follower of him. And that is the most important objective of the journey.

34
Arising from the Past Remanences

I opened my eyes. I was on the mataji's lap.
When I slept?
I tried to recollect things. I wake up from her lap and looked at
    her.
I am not remembering what had happened?
She smiled at me.
Nayamika, are you happy now?
Yeah mam, why you ask me?
Nothing beta. Go and catch your dreams.
A satisfied life is better than a successful life. For others you
    may be a failure, an unsuccessful person or a girl who
    earns less amount of money. But if you are happy, don't
    think back. The holy land needs you.
 I cant recollect the things happened around, am I in a past
    dream? But I feel weightlessness in my body or mind.
    like I feel I am floating in this holy air. I looked around
    chorabari is also got freezed for this much time? As I cant
    find any change in the eddies of chorabari, they are
    moving as the same pattern as I saw before I slept. I looked
    at mataji. How she can smile like this? Her smile is having
    a preternatural power.
I can see an aura around the head of mata ji. Is that an optical
    illusion, like a mirage on deserts? Did the sun hides
    behinds and that makes a constant scintillation around
    there? I scrutinized her.

She again moved her hands over me. In that rhythmic movement, unintentionally I closed my eyes.
I again deeply smell the holy sniff.
I opened my eyes.
Slowly turned around, as I conjectured, she was not there.
I didn't feel as I experienced a miracle.
I looked at the sun, it is going to cross the horizon, I will see the sun for two minutes after it crosses the horizon, I have seen mataji for a short interval of time and she disappears.
I smiled, as I know I have so many prodigies to experience if I follow my mind.I slowly walked through the mind, nothing hurts me, as there is spirit in my mind and it was deep rooted.
Listen your heart. There was an answer for the all the questions in your own mind. find it and enjoy the feeling of happiness, satisfaction, love the life.

35

Knowing about
her Destiny

I feel I was happy,satisfied than ever, but I didn't get the reason behind it. Soon as an intuition, I took my mobile, last few days it was switched off. I have seen some missed call notifications, among that three from divine home. I called back. The office lady Deepti attended the call

Oh sister Nayamika, I tried to contact you so many times. Oh, I was traveling, what happened?

There was an emergency here, on the next day you left here, one of our baba left us.

I prayed silently, God it won't be dev baba.

He felt some breathing issues and there was no alternative sister here and the hospital was 90 kms away from us.

Oh, I haven't know about that, sorry. I thought there will be some alternative nurses.

No madam, who will come and stay here in these fifteen degrees Celsius with this small amount of salary.

I didn't know about that Deepti.

Its fine madam, before your arrival there was only a nurse who visits here once in a month.

I am sorry. I feel a guilt in my mind.

No madam, I didn't call you to made you sorrowful, it's not your fault. before his death he has given a letter for you.

I got shivered. I am sure it will be dev baba. Before leaving there,I

must at least think about them. I should at least appoint an alternative nurse, I feel a pain in my heart.

They are the people who believed me, and what I did for them?I cut
the call, I didn't ask her the name of baba who died, I am
         sure that it is dev baba!
I sat there, pressed my head using by hands.
I have rescued him two three times from asthma breathing issues. If
I   was there, may I can help him from dying.
         I again feel a devotional trauma, God is trying to show you
      something. Try to find what your mind says, that is the
      god's vision for you. Every person born in this world is
      having a destiny. Some of them returned without finding
      them, but if you find it, life will a spectacular.
   In this life you have to face some incidents. that no one can
      change or go away from it. If you tried to go away from it,
         then it will follow you. Face it. I didn't upbraid myself for
         the death of dev baba. I feel a pain in heart and that pain
         changed my destiny.
I closed my eyes and the letter written by dev baba is visible
         now.
In his most beautiful calligraphy, with his blue parker
fountain pen, with a smile in his eyes he started writing. Each
word is becoming clearly visible for me. I smiled.

36
The life

Now I am seeing Piyush from a distance. As I saw him, I raised my hands and invites him to the place where I sit.I have seen a glory in his face, as he reached near to me and his eyes are sparkling and his cheeks are blushed with happiness.He sat near to me in a way he faces me.

Nayamika, I never try to leave you dear, I want to talk to you, I want to disclose what happened to me after that, for that I have waited.

I smiled at himand slowly comb his hair backwards with my hands, like a kid he sob, I have seen a drop of tears fell down from his eyes.

Nayamika, I can't live without you, I will become mad.

I smiled again.

He took my hands and bring it near to his lips and ready to kiss on my hands.

I drew back my hands.

He got annoyed.

Nayamika, I want you; I need you. Still you didn't believe me, I never try to cheat you dear, that day you left me, after that,

I placed my hands on his lips.

He looked at me with anxiety.

Piyush. I don't want to hear it.

So, what does it mean.? You believe me or not believe me

I believe you dear.

He smiled and adjust his position to come closer to me.

Then? You come with me, whatever happens or whoever against us that doesn't matter, I need you, I want you to be with me forever. I want to marry you. I never leave you nayamika. I promise.

I smiled at looked at the great Himalayas that spreads the holy spirit everywhere around it.

He looked at me with a strange face.

Say something Nayan.I am dying.

Piyush,

Say Nayamika, I am afraid while looking at your eyes. Piyush,I love you

she paused.

But now I am not the Nayamika you expects, more than our happiness, our life I have some other reasons to live.

Ok, that doesn't matter, you will have the freedom , I never oblige you for anything. we will care your family too, we will shift to kerala, if you want.

She smiled and he realized that that isn't the answer she expected.

Nayamika, please say what is in your mind.now I cant read you.

Piyush, you can understand me than no one else in this world.if I marry you , my life will completely dedicated to you and I will roam around you like how earth revolves around sun.

So, that is because you loves me. It will beautiful Nayan, our life.

There is an anticipation in his eyes.

But now, I don't want to follow a life like an ordinary women. I want to live for a group of persons who need my help and support.dev baba is no more and I must be there at divine home for its constant being and medical support. If I start loving you again, I will only think about you and will dedicate my life for you. And I will always afraid about the moment when you leave me. I will be constrained about being alone.

She paused for a moment.

There are some dadas and dadi s at divine home. May somebody will ask, what madness is that old people are doing, they can live at their own house by reading some holy books and waits for the arrival of death. But they left the home and staying at divine home happily, peacefully satisfactorily. I am also feeling an internal happiness there, a satisfaction, nothing can destroy that feeling as it was deep rooted.

I must be there Piyush. They need me.

I too need you Nayan.

But it is different.

He looked at me and I cant trace the feeling filled inside him.

Are you sure?

Yes Piyush. I decided it. I am going back to divine home.dev baba has given some duties for me, not duties, he makes clear my path,my destiny. Thank you Piyush for loving me like this.

He stood silently by looking at me.

I walked through the light snow rain that fell on me like flower rain. I am thankful to you god to help me to reach here, to make me happy,satisfied.

Nayamika, ek second?

I turned back,it was Piyush.

I know there is no doctors at your divine home, can I get a job there?

I smiled and open my hands and raise my face and enjoyed the snow rain that showered on me.

107 | Karthika S Nair